THE
TEMPLAR PIRATES

THE
TEMPLAR
PIRATES

THE SECRET ALLIANCE
TO BUILD THE NEW JERUSALEM

Ernesto Frers

Translated by Ariel Godwin

Destiny Books
Rochester, Vermont

Destiny Books
One Park Street
Rochester, Vermont 05767
www.DestinyBooks.com

Destiny Books is a division of Inner Traditions International

Originally published in Spanish under the title *Piratas y Templarios* by Ediciones
    Robinbook, Barcelona
First U.S. edition published in 2007 by Destiny Books

Library of Congress Cataloging-in-Publication Data
Frers, Ernesto.
    [Piratas y Templarios. English]
    The Templar pirates : the secret alliance to build the new Jerusalem /
Ernesto Frers ; translated by Ariel Godwin.
        p. cm.
    "Originally published in Spanish under the title Piratas y Templarios by
Ediciones Robinbook, Barcelona"—T.p. verso.
    Includes index.
    ISBN-13: 978-1-59477-146-0 (pbk.)
    ISBN-10: 1-59477-146-4 (pbk.)
    1. Templars—History. 2. Pirates—History. I. Title.
CR4749.F7413 2007
910.4'5dc22

                                                            2006038003

Printed and bound in Canada by Transcontinental

10   9   8   7   6   5   4   3   2

Text design and layout by Jon Desautels
This book was typeset in Sabon with Centaur as a display typeface

CONTENTS

Introduction: The Order of the Temple and Piracy   I

PART 1
BANDITS AND KNIGHTS

I The Dawn of Piracy   6
Imaginary Corsairs   7
Ancient Precursors   8
Boardings in the Aegean Sea   9
The Irony of Pompeius   12
The Vikings Are Coming!   17
The Normans Who Founded Russia   22
The Normans in Europe   22

2 The Mystery of the Order of the Temple   24
The Temple According to History   27
The Templars' Rise to Power   33
Persecution and Dispersion of the Order   37
The Lost Fleet of La Rochelle   41

PART 2
THE GOLDEN AGE OF PIRACY

3 The Temple and the Pirates   46
Pirates in the Mediterranean   46

The Thwarted Revenge of the Temple   49

Moors on the Coast   50

American Booty   51

The French Buccaneers   54

Huguenots and Templars   57

The Corsairs of the English Empire   60

    Francis Drake, the Queen's Corsair   61

    Henry Morgan, the Invincible Pirate   65

    William Kidd, the Scourge of the Indies   67

    The Terrible Edward Teach, or "Blackbeard"   70

    Bartholomew Roberts, the Fortunate   73

    "Calico Jack" and the Pirate Women   75

The Secret Presence of the Temple   80

The Templar Son of the Virgin Queen   82

4 The British Empire and the Privateers   84

The Vilification of the Corsairs   84

Sir Walter Raleigh and the Treasure of El Dorado   86

His Majesty's Informers   88

Under the Veil of the Royal Society   89

PART 3

THE ORDER OF THE TEMPLE AND FREEMASONRY

5 The Secret Lodge of the Stoneworkers   92

The Era of the Cathedrals   93

The Mythical Origins of Freemasonry   97

The British Connection   99

The Remarkable Rosslyn Chapel   103

The Illustrious Invisible College   104

Butting Heads with the Church   105

PART 4

THE TEMPLARS IN AMERICA

6 Voyages of Antiquity 108
The Megalithic Navigators 109
Solomon and the Phoenician Mariners 111
A Well-Known New World 113
The Route of the Codfish 114

7 The Templars' Transatlantic Voyage 115
The Secret of Oak Island 118
"Zeno's Narrative" 119
A Well-Hidden Treasure 122

8 The Mystery of Christopher Columbus 125
Kings and Navigators 128
A Happy Marriage 131
A Time of Setbacks 134
Columbus and the Promised Land 136
The Queen's Jewels 138
The Return of the Templars 139

9 In Search of New Arcadia 141
The Templar Port 143
The Voyage to Arcadia 146
Death in the Caribbean 148
The Signs of the Temple 148

10 Arcadia in Canada 152
The Navigators of the Order of Malta 152
The Knights of the Most Holy Sacrament 156
Mary Magdalene and the Black Virgin 158

11 Pirates and Freemasons in American Independence   160
    A Free Land for the "New Jerusalem"   160
    Freemasonry and the Thirteen Colonies   161
    The Privateers and the Revolution   165
    The Liberators and the Masonic Lodges   167
    Lafayette: Hero of Two Revolutions   168
    Masons and Revolutionaries in South America   169
    The Mysterious Retreat of Freemasonry   173
    Freemasonry versus Slavery   173

Conclusion   175

Index   179

THE ORDER OF
THE TEMPLE AND PIRACY

It might seem absurd or extravagant to claim that Templars and pirates maintained a close relationship. However, recent studies and discoveries have confirmed what unbiased historians and scholars of so-called secret societies have already believed for a long time: The alliance, complicity, and identification between the Templar knights and pirates went so far that apparently they even exchanged roles. Both Templars and pirates gained possession of some of the most powerful fleets in history, and they at least sailed in the same ships—or, better yet, were the same people. From the beginning of the fourteenth century onward, many Templars became pirates, and later, many famous pirates and corsairs observed the laws of the Temple or formed smaller lodges inspired by this order (such as the Brotherhood of the Coast in the Caribbean and the Libertalia sect in Madagascar).

In 1312, when the Vatican banned the Order of the Temple and confiscated all its possessions, holdings, and fortifications, the Templars—who were already excellent mariners—committed themselves permanently to the sea. Their immediate objective was very clear: to take revenge upon the pope and the Catholic kingdoms that served the Church. Their great fleet, moored at the French port of La Rochelle, vanished as if by magic. Later, after some transformations, which will be recounted, the "lost fleet" of the Temple reappeared, hoisting for the first time the dreaded black flag bearing the skull and crossbones. The Templar ships were dedicated largely to attacking the vessels of the Papal States and kingdoms allied with the Vatican, with the purpose of weakening the earthly powers of the Church. Since these powers were reflected in the flamboyant wealth of Rome and its allies, there was no shortage of spontaneous pirates willing to join the hunt for tempting booty. It is of no small significance that these autonomous bandits, serving the interests of the Temple in one way or another, were the prototype of the pirate coined by official history. The truth is that the actual founders and instigators of "modern" piracy were the Templars, first in the Mediterranean and later in the Atlantic and the Caribbean; they gave rise to the golden age of corsairs, buccaneers, and freebooters.

Navigators felt winds of independence and liberty blowing on the seas, and knew that the waters held ancient mysteries, that the waves were murmuring age-old secrets. On the great oceans, timeless and without masters, pirates and Templars influenced one another, building an ideology and a dream that left a mark on a large part of the later history of the Western world, and which probably even determined its future. The life of the pirate added a spirit of vitality and free will to the severe discipline of the Order of the Temple. The Templar knights, one must note, did not attack Catholic ships solely to take revenge on the pope, nor did they seize valuable treasure simply out of greed for riches. These actions formed part of a greater plan, which some scholars connect with the legend of Atlantis and lost sources of occult knowledge. Christian esotericism maintains that the Order held and guarded secrets such as the true identity of Jesus, his alleged marriage to Mary Magdalene, and the fate of the Holy Grail. Their ultimate, perhaps utopian objective was to establish a new universal order based on spirituality, humanism, and wisdom, possibly inspired by the memory of an ancient era. In the cryptic language of the Temple, this dreamed-of utopia was called the New Jerusalem.

With this secret objective, the Templar navigators fought a long battle against ruling dogmas and interests, symbolized by the Vatican as the seat of power and a materialistic deviation from the true evangelical message. Assuming that the ends justified the means, they used piracy, homicide, infiltration, espionage, and conspiracy to influence fundamental events of history, or to play the lead in them. These events were the geographical discoveries funded by the courts of Spain and Portugal, including the voyages of Christopher Columbus; the founding of Freemasonry as a civilian branch of the Temple; the peak of the age of Enlightenment; the outbreak of the French Revolution; the founding and independence of the United States of America, and its powerful navy; the emancipation of the Spanish colonies in America; the struggle of Garibaldi for the unification of Italy; and the triumph of the antislavery Union in the American Civil War.

In addition, the Templars acted as bankers in the High Middle Ages, financing thrones, wars, and crusades and granting loans to explorers and merchants that were later paid back into the castles and fortresses that the Order owned. When we add to this the valuable plunder obtained in their pirating raids, we can guess that the Templars possessed incalculable riches, only a small part of which was found and seized. It is probable that the fortune that the Templars hid, and the booty that the pirates buried, formed a fabulous common treasure, concealed in one or several places, the knowledge of which has been held by only a chosen few since then.

All the material in this book is based on confirmed historical data and the most recent investigations and studies on the subject, which combine with an abundant measure of intrigue, mystery, and the adventure that the subject offers to create an enjoyable and engaging text, stimulate the interest of the reader, and enrich his or her knowledge. I hope that I have been successful in this, and that these pages will answer to the axiom that, in the world and its history, "the truth is not always as it appears, but the truth is also not always apparent."

PART 1
BANDITS
AND KNIGHTS

1

THE DAWN OF PIRACY

When we hear the word *pirate,* we tend to think of a tough seaman with a plumed hat, a shirt with ruffles, musketeer boots, and an ample belly covered by a bandoleer over a coat with tassels. Or else we imagine the figure of the English corsair of the sixteenth through eighteenth centuries, embodied by Francis Drake, Henry Morgan, and the legendary Captain Kidd. Without a doubt, these personages and their era represent the golden age of piracy in the Western world, which gave fame and popularity to this intrepid and hazardous occupation. However, the history of piracy began much earlier, in distant antiquity, in scenes encompassing almost all the epochs and oceans of the world.

Piracy has been defined as any kind of criminal act on the sea, or "from the sea," since pirates often disembarked in order to raid coastal settlements and even committed their violent acts far inland. However, the greater part of their activity consisted of boarding and robbing other ships, preferably defenseless and with valuable cargo. The term is applied generally to lawless seamen who acted in their own interest and at their own risk, but also includes other categories, depending on the epoch and location of the activities or the nationality of the pirates and their relationship with their respective governments. The first French pirates of the Caribbean, who ate smoked meat *(viande boucanée),* were called *boucaners,* or "buccaneers"; pirates upon whom a king or governor conferred a license for their *corso* (Spanish for "piratical enterprise") were "corsairs"; shipowners and captains who acted as pirates in the name of a country but with private ships were called "privateers"; and seafarers of various nationalities and ethnicities who partnered together in order to sail freely in search of "booty" were called "freebooters," a term that passed to French as *flibustiers* and to Castilian Spanish as *filibusteros,* although in these languages it has more of a generic and literary use.

Spaniards, as the principal victims of the peak years of piracy, do not linger on these distinctions, considering them all words meaning "pirates"—not without good reason. But the English have resisted referring to the corsairs and privateers that way, and even awarded some of them titles of nobility or high positions in their navy. It is probable that this deference on the part of certain European kingdoms gave piracy an important status, linking it closely to the secret societies that exerted a decisive influence behind the throne. Thus some pirates and corsairs attained great power, wealth, and celebrity, thanks to their skills, their boldness, their ambition, and above all their good service to those in power, either openly or in secret. These exceptional men and women (some were indeed women, as we shall see) were involved in adventures and exploits that gave rise to the romantic legend of piracy.

Imaginary Corsairs

The pirate is one of the archetypes most mythologized and idealized in the arts, be it in poetry, literature, film, or comics. The romantic spirit of the nineteenth century was seduced by this extravagant and daring personage upon whom two conflicting models were conferred: that of the young swordsman, handsome and quick to fall in love, fighting against the abuse of power like a Robin Hood of the seas; and that of the sinister thug without scruples, enhancing his villainous role with an eye patch, a hook for a hand, and a wooden leg as a simple prosthetic.

The truth is that the real pirates were neither so charming nor so execrable. Led by successful captains, the typical crew of pirates was made up of small-time adventurers, ex-combatants, mutinous sailors, deserters, fugitives from the law, and escaped slaves seeking a refuge and a livelihood. Recruited from the margins of society, many hoped to become rich from the fabulous booty talked about in the taverns—wealth that in reality was neither abundant nor easily obtained. Those with eye patches and hooks were not merely invented by Robert Louis Stevenson in *Treasure Island* or by James Barrie in *Peter Pan;* such things were the consequences of mutilations in hand-to-hand combat or accidents on board. Nor was their immoderate liking for rum—a liquor from the West Indies distilled from sugarcane, very easy to make and very intoxicating—purely the product of literature. Its alcohol content of nearly 75 percent wreaked havoc on constitutions already weakened by malnutrition and tropical fevers and infections.

Nevertheless, these coarse sailors were the cannon fodder that made possible the naval battles, boardings, and sackings that bestowed fame upon the great corsairs and influenced the politics and economics of this era of history. For them, piracy held two great attractions: on the one hand, a communal lifestyle and some models of conduct that were more free and egalitarian than any of the laws of the time; on the other hand, participation in a secret project to free humanity from its miseries, a transcendent and occult plan, the true knowledge of which could not be attained but that gave meaning to their lives.

Ancient Precursors

More than four millennia ago, Egyptian and Phoenician ships were the targets of actions that can be classified as piracy. At that time, these same activities were already common in the waters of the Indian Ocean, in the seas around China, and along the coasts of Southeast Asia. As for the Mediterranean, the oldest relevant document is a clay tablet dated to 1350 BC from the Egyptian island of Pharos, which mentions attacks by Berber pirates on the African coast. Later, Greek merchants trading between Phoenicia and Anatolia frequently reported the boarding and sacking of their ships.

It can be safely said that ever since the first seafarers began to transport property and merchandise, other seafarers dedicated themselves to attacking them and seizing their cargo. Initially, these robber mariners limited themselves to imitating the practices of highwaymen on dry land, and in fact many of them were simply bandits who embarked with the intent of sacking small ports and riverside villages. With the passage of time, their activities acquired specific resources and tactics, adapting to advances in navigation and the expansion and diversification of maritime routes. This era gave rise to the image of the pirate as the criminal of the sea, specializing in attacking merchant vessels but not giving up on robbing coastal populations. Their methods and resources developed in accordance with naval history and the growing importance and influence of seafaring in commerce, politics, war, and the competition between nations.

Boardings in the Aegean Sea

The first manifestation of organized piracy in Europe with notable economic and political consequences occurred in the sixth century BC on the island of Samos. In the middle of that century, a party of adventuring sailors landed there, coming from Magnesia under the command of three brothers hardened by sea skirmishes and fighting in the resistance against the Persians. Encountering no resistance from the terrified inhabitants, the invaders seized the city, toppling the current governor and his minions in the local oligarchy. Now owners of the island, the brothers established a triumvirate government. In order to impose their authority in the region, the cruelest and most ambitious of the three, Polycrates, organized pirating expeditions to the nearest islands and coasts. To prove the effectiveness of this method for subjugating the locals and obtaining valuable plunder, Polycrates conceived the idea of extending this pillaging throughout the Aegean Sea, making Samos into a true pirate state. His two brothers were opposed to this, although it is not known whether for ethical reasons or doubts about the possibility of success. In any case, they did not reckon with the obstinacy and ferocity of Polycrates, who was blindly intent on having his way. During the celebration of the feast of the goddess Hera, which took place outside the city walls, Polycrates and his pirate captains took possession of the palace. After seizing power, the new tyrant quickly removed his triumviral brothers, killing one and exiling the other after accusing them of treason—the usual excuse in such cases at the time.

Polycrates immediately assumed absolute power, proclaiming an individual and lifelong tyranny, which was sustained by the booty from his pirate ships. The tyrant of Samos knew that the best way of discouraging any attempt to attack his island was to display an imposing naval power, both in the Aegean and along the coasts of the Peloponnesus and Asia Minor. He organized a formidable pirate fleet of more than a hundred ships, which deployed in speedy and effective flotillas, spreading terror throughout Greece for the next fifty years. Besides keeping his terrified neighbors at bay, these continual raids enriched the coffers of Samos and the personal fortune of its fearsome governor.

Having become virtual master of the Aegean, Polycrates was forced to take into account the other two great maritime powers of the era: Persia to the east and Egypt to the south. In principle, he made an agreement with Pharaoh Amasis to divide the dominion of the eastern Mediterranean so that the Egyptian ships would protect his fleets during their pirating expeditions. However, Persia also aspired to rule these waters, and therefore started a naval war with Egypt in 525 BC. The pharaoh, thinking he could count on his Greek ally, found that Polycrates not only abandoned him without letting him know, but also became his enemy. The pirate tyrant, an expert in such disputes, had calculated that the Egyptians did not have sufficient forces to oppose the powerful Persian fleet, and that if they attempted to do so, they would be defeated. He did not hesitate to act accordingly, going over to the side of the more likely victor. However, his abusive absolutism had made him enemies among his own captains, and rumors of an imminent rebellion flew around the streets and markets of Samos. Polycrates formed a plan in which he could kill two birds with one stone: He would send a squadron of forty ships to join the Persian fleet and place his discontented captains right at the front of this expedition. However, these captains decided that this was not their war, so instead of joining the Persian fleet, they directed their squadron's course to Sparta, seeking help in overthrowing Polycrates.

The austere and warlike Spartans had succeeded in forming the Confederation of the Peloponnesus in order to resist the Persian invasions. If Sparta collaborated in the defeat of Polycrates, the Persian fleet would lose a valuable backup and Sparta would gain prestige in the view of its own allies, habitual victims of the pirates of Samos. These, at least, were the arguments made by the deserters from Samos before the Council of Sparta, which resolved to provide them with prudent and secret aid in the form of arms and sailors. But Polycrates, informed by his spies, thwarted the rebel invasion just after they landed on the island. The ringleaders were executed at once, and their accomplices imprisoned as slaves. The hundred pirate ships of the tyrant of Samos kept on ravaging the seas of Greece, but just for a few more years.

Not only did the pharaoh feel betrayed by Polycrates in his war against Persia, but so also did the Persians themselves, when the promised squadron from Samos never arrived to join their fleet. In 522 BC, the new emperor of Persia, Darius I, ordered Oroetes, the satrap of Sardis, to lure Polycrates to his palace with the promise of entrusting a very well-paid naval operation to him. The formidable pirate fell into the trap; he was arrested immediately and condemned to death by crucifixion.

Despite what one might imagine, Polycrates was not a brutal and ignorant dictator. On the contrary, he was a cultured man and a sensitive governor, concerned with the well-being and prosperity of his subjects, promoting education and generously patronizing literature and the arts. Among the figures who shone forth in his court were the famous poet Anacreon (whose odes to love and life's pleasures influenced Renaissance poets) and various artists and philosophers who enjoyed the patronage of this pirate-turned-ruler. This attraction of pirates to culture was not unusual in the greater part of their history.

Only a narrow channel separates the mountainous island of Samos from the Ionian coast of Asia Minor, where the prosperous city of Ephesus lay under the power of imperial Persia during this epoch. About twelve kilometers to the south, on the banks of the river Meandros, was the Thessalian enclave of Magnesia, eternal rival of Ephesus and a river port that played an important role in the development of navigation and naval war in classical Greece. The key character in one example of this was Themistocles, an Athenian politician and strategist of the fifth century BC who decided to form a great fleet in order to cut off the maritime supplies of the Persian army. With this purpose, he turned to Magnesia's expert shipbuilders, who built two hundred new combat ships with three tiers of oars on each side (triremes), which formed the first Attic war fleet of such a great size. Leading this fleet, Themistocles not only put an end to the hegemony of the squadrons of Xerxes I, but also dealt some hard blows to Xerxes' Phoenician allies.

After the unfortunate end of Polycrates' adventures, pirates prudently reduced their presence in the waters of the Mediterranean. Every now and then, a pirate vessel would attack a defenseless Greek or Persian ship in order to appropriate its provisions and a few amphoras of oil, sacks of grain, or skins of wine, which would later be resold in clandestine markets. This sort of piracy for survival originated in certain ports in Asia Minor and among the Berbers along the coast of the Maghreb on the northwest coast of Africa, who would terrorize the whole Mediterranean some centuries later.

For now, the eastern Mediterranean was the scene of some of the most spectacular and decisive battles in Western history. The latent hostility and competition between Athens and Sparta exploded in the spring of 430 BC when the Spartans attacked Plataea, a city allied with the Athenians. Pericles, the Attic strategist, decided not to confront the powerful invading army on land, but instead to entice Sparta to fight the war at sea. The two sides soon filled the Aegean Sea with armed ships, greatly superior to the modest vessels used by the impromptu pirates of the epoch. Piracy became too risky an occupation, and quickly dwindled almost to disappearance.

Half a century later, the formidable campaigns of Alexander the Great—who gained power over Asia Minor, Persia, Egypt, and almost the entire world known to the West—eliminated any possibility for piracy in the waters and along the coasts that the young Macedonian conqueror's armies controlled. Shortly afterward, in 264 BC, a well-known and persistent struggle began between Rome and Carthage for the control of the Mediterranean, and the sea was caught between the two combatants, its waters infested by new and numerous battleships. These Punic Wars, with their variable success and unfulfilled truces, went on for almost two hundred years, until the definitive victory of the Romans in 146 BC. For two long centuries, potential pirates of the area remained peacefully on dry land.

The Irony of Pompeius

In the first century BC, when Rome was at the beginning of its age of greatest splendor, the Pax Romana had reduced the necessity of maintaining armed vigilance at sea. At the same time, the busy comings and goings of cargo ships full of costly merchandise revived the greed of pirates from the Levant (on the eastern coast of the Mediterranean) and Africa, who embarked upon raids and boardings in search of this valuable booty. The Roman governors, busy with internal quarrels and inland conquests, paid no attention to the phenomenon until mare nostrum (our sea) was practically in the power of the pirates.

The pirates' favorite places of operations were the maritime routes connecting Rome and the rest of Italy with Africa and Spain to the west and with the provinces of Macedonia, Greece, Syria, and Egypt to the east. A busy traffic of rich merchandise was there for the taking. Almost all the pirate ships came from the coast of Cilicia (now southwest Turkey), whose convoluted shoreline offered numerous safe ports and hidden anchorages. The most important hideout was the Gulf of Alexandretta, across from the nearby island of Cyprus, where the pirates set up their main headquarters, taking advantage of the decadence of the Seleucid kingdoms of Syria and Rhodes. Rome had annexed these territories at the beginning of the second century BC, but its distracted administration had relaxed its control over the waters and coastlines of this region.

From then on, piracy reigned at will in the Mediterranean, to the point that the governors of coastal cities and provinces, unprotected by Rome, resorted to establishing treaties with the pirate chiefs. In these agreements, they offered tributes, provisions, and refuge in exchange for not being attacked, with the result that the whole perimeter of mare nostrum was dotted with secure enclaves of piracy. Encouraged by such impunity, several captains landed at the mouth of the Tiber in 68 BC and advanced by land almost to the gates of Rome. Rome, at the same time, sent out a cohort to keep them at bay. The pirates returned to their ships and formed a barrier in the Tyrrhenian Sea, preventing the passage of vessels transporting essential provisions from the colonies.

This episode highlighted the severity of the problem, and Rome, besieged almost to the point of starvation, had to find a solution. To this end, she called up the prestigious general Gnaeus Pompeius—highly experienced at pulling the Republic's chestnuts out of the fire, having already defeated the rebel general Sertorius in Spain and suppressed the great slave revolt led by Spartacus. Eliminating the pirates turned out to be child's play for him. The Senate authorized him to prepare two hundred warships and conceded to him the exceptional authority of personally holding levies to augment his army. A conscientious and methodical warrior, Pompeius divided mare nostrum and its coasts into two zones, west and east, which in their turn were subdivided into several sectors. His fleet then began to sweep west across the Levant, one sector after the next, and after only forty days had cleared the first zone of every last ship, captain, and individual pirate. He then advanced upon the eastern part, and some six weeks later arrived in Cilicia, which, after a few punitive operations, he incorporated as a Roman province.

This impressive operation elevated Gnaeus Pompeius to even higher fame, and he stayed in Cilicia, dividing up land among repentant pirates and retraining them as peasants. While he was there, and perhaps to keep him at a safe distance, Rome granted him supreme power to pacify and organize all his territories and frontiers in Asia Minor. The efficient strategist carried out this complex mission to perfection, and later

After his defeat at Pharsalia, Pompeius fled to Egypt, where he was assassinated in his ship by order of King Ptolemy XIII. (Engraving by B. Pinelli, 1819.)

repeated the feat in Africa. From that time, his legions began calling him Pompeius "the Great," imitating the moniker of Alexander. Later, Pompeius formed the first triumvirate with Crassus and Julius Caesar, becoming a major obstacle to Caesar's ambitions. During the civil war between him and Caesar, Pompeius was assassinated in Egypt in 48 BC. His younger son, Sextus Pompeius Pius, an impulsive nineteen-year-old youth, took up his mantle.

After the crafty assassination of his father, Sextus was proclaimed successor and commander of the scant troops who remained faithful to the Pompeian cause. Before Caesar's triumph, in 45 BC, Sextus fled to Spain without renouncing his legacy and fought with the Roman garrisons stationed on the Iberian Peninsula. Caesar was assassinated by a conspiracy led by Brutus and Cassius on the ides of March in the following year. The conspirators fled the public's anger at their crime and formed a new triumvirate, led by Marcus Antonius. The latter, deciding to avenge the death of his patron, made an agreement with

Marble bust of Julius Caesar, who wrote The Gallic Wars *as a chronicle of the campaign of his legions in conquest of the territory of Gaul.*

Sextus Pompeius that granted the young man command of a squadron for controlling the Western Mediterranean. However, Sextus used the ships to consolidate his own dominion over the coasts of Spain. In view of this act of contempt, Marcus Antonius revoked his command and declared him an outlaw.

It is probable that Sextus embraced his status as outlaw cheerfully, since it left him free to attack Roman possessions at whim. His ships formed an intimidating pirate fleet that ravaged and blockaded the Italian peninsula for several years. His greatest operation was the occupation of the island of Sicily in 39 BC, which forced Marcus Antonius to establish a new agreement; Sextus assisted him in his struggle against Octavian (the future emperor Augustus) in exchange for being designated official governor of Sicily and other smaller islands. The designation never came about, despite the pirate ships' harassing those of Octavian and successfully carrying out several skirmishes. But in 36 BC, Marcus Agrippa, at the head of a large fleet, thoroughly defeated Sextus Pompeius on the Sicilian coast. The vanquished pirate initiated a retreat to Asia Minor, but was captured and executed shortly afterward.

THE PRINCESS AND THE PIRATES

The *Aethiopica* is an account by Heliodorus of Emesa, a Greek writer in the third century AD, of the epic journey of Princess Chariclea, daughter of the king of Ethiopia. Abandoned by her mother at birth and ignorant of her origin, Chariclea grew up in Delphi. There she met a young Thessalian named Theagenes. The two of them fell in love, and he decided to escort her on her return to her true home. On the way, they were captured by pirates, who held them captive in separate places. The main part of the story consists of the efforts of the two lovers to escape and reunite. All ended well: The pirates were tricked, and the king of Ethiopia gave up his throne to his daughter and blessed her marriage to Theagenes, who became a rich and powerful prince. This story reveals the importance of pirates in this epoch; they were sufficiently well known to play the role of villains in a popular Byzantine narrative.

It is no small irony that Sextus Pompeius, the most notorious Roman pirate, was the son and heir of the man who, some years earlier, had distinguished himself by eliminating piracy in the Mediterranean.

The Vikings Are Coming!

The Western Roman Empire collapsed in the second half of the fifth century AD. The two main causes of its fall were the deterioration of its internal unity and invasions by people whom the Greco-Latin world had scornfully referred to as "barbarians." This phenomenon was accompanied by a great migration of people from the Eurasian plains (Suevi, Vandals, Alans, Franks, and Ostrogoths) and some of the northern steppes of Asia (Huns and Avars). The majority of them were skilled horsemen and fearsome fighters, but because of their geographic origin, they had no knowledge of seafaring or of any other mariners' arts. The Mediterranean therefore held no great interest for Europe's new masters, whose principal economy had no need for the complex network of maritime routes that the Romans had established. Seafaring dwindled in all the seas of Europe, and with it the valuable cargoes that had been the reason for piracy to take place. Only the tireless Berber pirates kept up their work in the waters of Asia Minor, where the ships of the flourishing Byzantine Empire still offered tempting spoils.

While the barbarian kingdoms established in Europe fought among themselves with their backs to the sea, seafaring received a new boost in far-off Scandinavia. The indigenous Lappish and Gothic populations had already been conquered and partly assimilated by invaders of Germanic origin. This process generated a combative and highly seaworthy people who called themselves Vikings, meaning apparently "kings of the sea" in their language. Given the extensive convoluted and fjord-lined coastlines that characterize the area, shipbuilding was a natural occupation for them, and seafaring their principal activity. The Vikings excelled in both, and the inhospitable climate, together with their adventurous spirit, led them to seek new horizons at sea.

We know about the voyage of Erik the Red, who reached the shores of Greenland at the end of the tenth century, and that of his sons Leif and Thorvald, who landed in North America a few years later on the coast of what is now Nova Scotia. For these exploits, the Viking mariners used relatively large ships, between sixteen and twenty-four meters (fifty and seventy-five feet) long, with a single movable square sail, which made them very seaworthy. For trading voyages along the coasts and to the nearby islands, they used their swiftest and most maneuverable vessels, the *drakkars* (dragons), with polished hulls and no keel, which allowed them to sail in shallow waters and penetrate winding rivers and fjords.

The first great pirate-style invasion by the Vikings took place AD 793, when a few drakkars arrived, almost by accident, on the island of Lindisfarne, on the northwest coast of Britain. This island was known as the Holy Island because the monastery of Saint Cuthbert, the origin of the Gospel of Lindisfarne, had been built there two centuries earlier; it was the masterwork of the type of enlightenment attained by the Saxon monks. The brotherhood of Saint Cuthbert was rich and influential, owning valuable objects of worship and receiving generous donations in gold, silver, and precious stones. The Vikings destroyed everything in their way, including the terrified and defenseless monks, and returned to their ships with a fabulous cargo of booty. News of the successful invasion of Lindisfarne spread rapidly through Scandinavian villages and ports, increasing the Vikings' ambition and inclination toward exodus from their settlements in those nearly polar lands.

Thus began one of the greatest epochs of piracy in history, as the Vikings spread terror all over Europe for more than two hundred years, establishing themselves throughout a good part of it and playing an important role in the consolidation of the peoples and nations that form the continent today. Their primary victims, the Angles and Saxons of the British Isles, called the Vikings "north seamen" because their distinctive sails and threatening dragon-headed prows would typically emerge from this cardinal point on the horizon. The term evolved into Norsemen in English and passed on to the Romance languages as Normans, a name later given to the Viking populations permanently settled in Europe.

In the first few years after the sacking of Lindisfarne, the northern pirates carried out only seasonal raids, pillaging everything they could along the coasts of Britain, Ireland, and France, then returning home afterward. Each appearance caused an outbreak of panic: The nobles locked themselves up in their castles and the common people sought

The prows of Viking ships, decorated with dragon figureheads, must have caused great terror among the inhabitants of the British Isles as they emerged out of the fog.

Impression of a Viking ship, from a Norwegian illustration, 1911.

divine shelter in the churches, where the invaders slaughtered them en masse—at least they had a chance to confess their sins first. The churches were sacked not for any malicious pagan religious reasons, but merely because they were the seats of true power at the time, and therefore the places where the riches were stored. The Vikings methodically plundered churches and monasteries along the British and French coasts almost every year, in addition to the villages and farms of the surrounding areas.

Viking pirates did not rely solely on terror and blood for their livelihood. When they could, they also made use of their maritime voyages to barter or trade merchandise, sometimes with the same villages that they had sacked earlier. Their products consisted of furs, horns, walrus tusks, wood carvings, and runic stones with decorative motifs. But it was not rare for them to sell gold and slaves, taken from English monasteries, in Danish ports. The bishops and feudal lords took note of this mercantile practice of the vicious pirates, and made an agreement with them. The treaty consisted of paying the Vikings a high annual tribute in exchange for their not sacking and razing the churches and coastal settlements. Eventually the pirates grew tired of going back and forth across the rough, freezing waters of the North Sea, and began to settle in the territories they had invaded. First there were only armed fortifications and port enclaves, but little by little these were surrounded by villages and farmland cultivated by Scandinavian colonies. These

Viking banquet, from a medieval manuscript.

colonies flourished in the Faeroe and Shetland Islands, northern Scotland, northern Ireland, and Yorkshire, but their greatest settlements were in northwestern France, in the region that was named Normandy for this reason. There was also a brief Norman empire in the eleventh century, comprising Sweden, Denmark, and England, and a fearsome reign of Viking pirates in Sicily, which they invaded in 1061.

The Normans Who Founded Russia

While the Vikings set about invading Europe, another Scandinavian people, the Varangians, emigrated to the east. More disposed to commerce than to war, the Varangians crossed the Baltic and entered the continent, establishing various merchant colonies. Halfway through the ninth century, the Varangian tribe of the Rus settled on the banks of the Volga to secure the river commerce between the Baltic and Black Seas. The Slavic populations, terrorized by the Mongol hordes, asked for the protection of the Rus chief Riurik, who founded the principality of Novgorod in 860. His son, Prince Oleg, moved the capital to Kiev, in Ukraine, to facilitate commerce with Constantinople. The Varangians were thus the founders of the first Russian state. They gave the name of their tribe to this enormous region, imposed orthodox Christianity, and opened the way for its gradual incorporation into European culture.

The Normans in Europe

Meanwhile, in the north, the primitive Scandinavian tribes had organized themselves into two great kingdoms in imitation of what they had seen in Europe, perhaps to administer their wealth more effectively. At the end of the tenth century, Harald I Harfager was the first king of Norway and Harald II Batland occupied the throne of Denmark, which, although separated from Sweden by the Strait of Kattegat, has always been considered part of Scandinavia because of its history and culture. Both monarchs gave in to the pressures of Christianity, and this conversion was the beginning of the end of Viking piracy.

By the beginning of the second millennium, French Normandy had become an important feudal duchy, paying a sporadic vassalage to the king of France. In 1035, William the Bastard, son of Duke Robert I, persuaded the Norman barons to accept him as his father's successor, despite his being an illegitimate son and of only half Viking blood. The new duke was the cousin of Edward the Confessor, king of England, who had left no descendants. Upon Edward's death in 1066, his brother-in-law Harald, Earl of Essex, was proclaimed heir to high Anglo-Saxon nobility; but the Norman duke immediately arrived on the English coast with an armed mob, citing an old promise made by Edward naming William as his successor. The armies of the two contenders met on the outskirts of the city of Hastings. William wanted to take the throne without any bloodshed, and was also uncle-in-law to Harald, who he proposed should divide up England amicably. When the Norman emissary asked the king which territories he would hand over to the duke, Harald responded, "I promise him six feet of good English land!" The phrase became famous, but the one who ended up six feet under was Harald, defeated and killed in this Battle of Hastings. The victor quickly headed for Westminster, where in the abbey he was crowned king on Christmas Day 1066. Thus William the Bastard was converted by history into William the Conqueror, and the Anglo-Saxons lost the throne of England forevermore. The Norman dynasty reigned for three centuries, during which the Britannic kingdom was definitively established.

In northern Germany around the end of the twelfth century, a new merchant bourgeoisie arose and settled in towns on or near the coast of the Baltic Sea. Among these towns were Hamburg, Lübeck, Rostock, Wismar, and Danzig: in all, twenty-nine cities principally dedicated to commerce. When Viking pirates and highwaymen threatened their sea and land trading with Russia and the cities of eastern Europe, in 1158 they formed a defensive federation known as the Hansa Teutonica. The martial section of this league was the Order of Teutonic Knights, which later enlisted early Templars, fugitives from the stake burnings of the Inquisition.

This alliance of merchants resulted quickly in the extinction of the Nordic pirates, who had not obtained the kingdoms, fleets, and armies they wanted. The Hanseatic League forced new Scandinavian monarchs to give up invading with their Viking ships, which were already becoming obsolete.

2

THE MYSTERY
OF THE ORDER OF
THE TEMPLE

At the beginning of the thirteenth century, amid the Crusaders' short-lived occupation of the Holy Land, two orders emerged that were both monastic and knightly. The first was that of the Knights Hospitaller of Saint John (later the Order of Malta), who were strictly obedient to the pope. Shortly afterward, the Order of the Knights of the Temple arose in Jerusalem, characterized by its independence from the leaders of the Crusades as well as from the current pope. Both orders of warrior monks would have been no more than a footnote in the chronicle of this intense and tumultuous epoch had it not been for the enormous power and wealth that the Templars acquired. The Order of the Temple played the role of a virtual state within many European kingdoms, often as an intangible power behind the throne. The fact that the Temple ended up being suppressed by the pope and condemned by the Inquisition only amplified the aura of mystery and legend surrounding it; this aura increased even more with the alleged, and sometimes indubitable, presence of the Templars later on in transcendent historical places and events.

In addition to discussing the fate of the "lost fleet" of the Temple, and the intervention of the Templars in the voyages of Christopher Columbus and the independence of the United States—which are certainly controversial subjects in terms of concrete historical events—several authors and researchers ascribe an enigmatic origin to the Templars (everything

The Grand Master of the Hospitaller Knights of Saint John kneels and prays before John the Baptist, who holds the platter of the grail depicting the Pascal Lamb.

from the brotherhood of Phoenician seafarers to an antediluvian and even extraterrestrial genesis), and attribute to them a mysterious millenary project. This project could just as well be the triumph of a diabolical evil empire as the establishment of a wise and just world order. In either case, its realization necessarily required the extermination of the Vatican and the destruction of the Roman Catholic Church.

To correctly situate the creation and early history of the Order of the Temple, we should review the historical events that made these actions possible and set the scene for their emergence: the European invasions of the Levant in the eleventh and twelfth centuries, known as the Crusades. At the Council of Clermont-Ferrand in 1095, Pope Urban II delivered a passionate harangue calling upon the monarchs and nobles of Europe to fight a holy war. The objective was to liberate the Christian prisoners enslaved by the Muslims and seize the Holy Sepulchre. However, these noble goals concealed expansionist and economic interests—those of the Vatican, just as much as those of the European kings and nobles.

Images of crusaders. The image on the right, from the Church of the Temple in London, has long been thought to represent Geoffrey de Mandeville, who died in 1144.

The First Crusade, led by an alliance of feudal knights, was the only successful one. In 1099, the chief crusader Godfrey de Bouillon entered Jerusalem, completing the conquest of a large territory that was then divided into four Christian enclaves designated "Latin States": the Kingdom of Palestine, with its court in Jerusalem; the Kingdom of Syria, with its capital in Antioch; and the counties of Tripoli (now Libya) and Edessa (now Turkey). In this hostile territory, under an unstable occupation, emerged a religious and knightly order that would become the most powerful and controversial in history. The aforementioned states,

Templar knights attacking the walls of Jerusalem in 1099.

weakened and surrounded by adversaries, could not protect the thousands of pilgrims who flocked to the Holy Land along highways lined with bandits and sporadic enemy gangs. This was the reason, or at least the pretext, for creating this order, capable of offering travelers both military protection and spiritual guidance.

The Temple According to History

Setting aside for the moment the Hermetic and esoteric connotations that surround the Order of the Temple, we will examine the real and concrete facts properly documented and confirmed by scholars and researchers of academic ranking.

Official history records that in 1118, nine disheveled French knights led by Hughes de Payns presented themselves before Baldwin II, sovereign of the Latin Kingdom of Jerusalem, desiring to offer him their services. Their proposition was to establish a religious and military order to defend

Medieval miniature depicting crusading knights on their way to the Holy Land.

the Holy Places and provide protection for the pilgrims passing along the dangerous highways of the Holy Land. The king, perhaps touched by the generous objective of this group of veteran crusaders, offered them lodging in an old building adjacent to the mosque of the Dome of the Rock, built on the site of the ancient Temple of Solomon. Those living nearby, having seen the frugality and poverty of these ragged men who intended to form a knightly order, called them "the poor knights of the Temple." Little is known of the original nine knights who founded the Order, and even less is known of their true motives. The chronicles preserve the names of five of them, but not their lineage or previous history. It is known only that they were all, or almost all, of French origin and veterans of the First Crusade, and it is suspected that one of them might have been a Norman called Saint Clair. At a very young age, this knight had fought valiantly alongside Godfrey de Bouillon, and as we shall see later, his descendant played a fundamental role in the later history of the Temple. After the capture of Jerusalem, the majority of the nobles who had participated in the conquest returned to Europe to rest on their respective laurels and attend to their duties. Only the more fanatical, or those who lacked funds to return, remained in the Latin States. It is pos-

The Dome of the Rock and the Temple of Solomon in Jerusalem, illustrated in an antique engraving.

sible that Hughes de Payns and his companions shared both conditions, considering they were not lacking in fanaticism and their means of living revolved around mendicancy.

A little time after its foundation, the group acquired a tenth member, Count Hugh de Champagne, a French noble very well connected in the court and ecclesiastic circles. It is possible that through the intermediary of this influential aristocrat, the founders of the Temple made contact with the wise and mysterious monk Bernard de Clairvaux, one of the most fascinating and obscure characters of Christian hagiography. The future saint Bernard had six years previously written the rule of the new

Saint Bernard was one of the Benedictine monks who fought hardest to reestablish the rule of Saint Benedict.

TEMPLARS IN PAIRS

The founding Templars numbered fewer than ten, and their cavalry was scanter still. In fact, it was not uncommon in the streets of Jerusalem to see two stern knights mounted upon a single steed, and they tended to travel, eat, and fight in pairs, at least in the early times. This curious custom raised some suspicions among the crowds of Jerusalem, and was the object of mockery at the hands of the soldiers and the other crusading knights, especially those belonging to the rival order of the Hospitallers of Saint John. Almost two centuries later, in the tendentious proceedings of the court of the Inquisition, the Order of the Temple was accused, among other crimes, of "practicing sodomy."

Two Templars mounted on a single steed, depicted in a miniature from a medieval manuscript.

Cistercian monastic brotherhood, intending to recapture the austerity and spirituality that the original order of Cluny had lost as it succumbed to worldly ostentation. A little before the time of the creation of the Temple, Bernard held a secret meeting with the Templar leaders Champagne and de Payns, who asked him for his advice regarding the organization and foundation of the Order. The abbot of Clairvaux showed great interest in the initiative of the knightly monks and, besides establishing the foundations of the Rule of the Temple, promised them that he would

Scene of the Inquisition, by Francisco de Goya.

arrange with the pope for the recognition and pontifical consecration of the Order. It was also he who suggested the use of the characteristic cloak with a white front, to be distinguished from the black clothing of the Hospitallers, and the emblematic cross, red in color, with two points on each arm, which the Templars wore on their chests at the location of the heart.

The Rule of the Order of the Temple, inspired by Saint Bernard, included the usual vows of obedience, poverty, and chastity, to which the knights surely adhered strictly. The rule added the obligations to give alms to indigents, attend mass, and eat meat at least three times a week in order to maintain the spiritual health and physical strength necessary for the proper accomplishment of the knights' mission. At the same time, a series of rules was bound together with the knightly oath, among them those of aiding another Templar in distress, even at risk of losing one's life; of entering into combat with up to three enemies at a time; and of not responding to any provocation from another Christian knight unless he delivered his challenge three times over. The violation of these precepts was punished by three hard consecutive whippings. Needless to say, the number three held great symbolism for the Templars.

Bernard de Clairvaux finally kept his promise to obtain pontifical consecration for the new Order. In a council prepared by Bernard himself,

Templar knight with the white habit and red cross characteristic of the Order.

which met at Troyes in 1128, Pope Honorius II approved, and proclaimed with all due pomp, the institution of the Order of the Knights of Christ and the Temple of Jerusalem, designating the founder, Hughes de Payns, as its first Grand Master. Both Bernard and the Count of Champagne stayed in the shadows; they had their reasons for doing so.

The Templars' Rise to Power

In the following years, the Temple grew at a surprising rate, both in the number of its knights and in its possessions and monetary endowment. To become a Templar and take the vow of poverty, the aspirant had to give his castle and feudal properties to the Order, as well as the benefits from the use of his lands, which went to buy weapons, shields, warhorses, armor, and other equipment. But the Order's wealth did not come solely from the donations of the new knights, but also from the generous contributions of monarchs, princes, nobles, and rich merchants and traders connected with the Priory of Sion.

In 1146, the Muslims retook the beleaguered Latin state of Edessa, giving rise to the Second Crusade, which the young and inept French king Louis VII led to a resounding failure. The Muslim counteroffensive, led by the shrewd sultan Saladin, defeated the defenses of Jerusalem in 1187, expelling the Christian invaders from the Holy Land. The Templars were skeptical regarding the Third Crusade, organized by Richard the Lionheart and Philip Augustus of France; they steered clear of this campaign, favored by Pope Clement III, thus aggravating their differences with the Vatican. Acting openly on their own, they fought with the factions of the intermittent internal war among the Muslim kingdoms as well as with Christian groups. Chronicles tell of repeated bloody encounters with the terrifying Nazari Islamic sect of the Assassins (or *ashhashin*, hashish addicts), and ferocious combat with the Papal order of the Hospitallers of Saint John, with favorable results for the Temple.

After a brief stay on the island of Cyprus, the Templars moved to Europe and set up their headquarters in Paris, establishing important operative centers in Catalonia, Aragon, and the south of France, the home of the Cathars, founders of the Merovingian dynasty.

Having more than enough arms and resources for their mission,

Christian crusader knights attacking their Muslim opponents, whom they nevertheless respected for their valor as warriors.

In the twelfth century, the Templar order built a practically autonomous fortified area north of the Marais in Paris. In 1313, the walled district of the Templars passed to the Order of Malta, until the Revolution of 1789. (L'Enclos du Temple, anonymous fifteenth-century painting.)

the Templars did not end up using all the money and goods that their Order continually received. They therefore organized a sort of medieval bank, which they operated in two modes: On the one hand, they lent considerable sums to sovereigns and great nobles, both to assist their troubled finances and to pay the high costs of wars and invasions; on the other hand, by using their castles and enclaves in almost all the known world, they established a credit system for voyagers and merchants, who in this way could undertake long voyages without having to carry all their money with them. To attend to its numerous commercial activities and mercantile exchanges, the Temple possessed a large fleet of modern ships, whose main base was the French port of La Rochelle.

One of the many surprising facts in the history of the Templars relates to their considerable architectural knowledge, which made them influential in the rise of the Gothic style in the twelfth century. It seems certain that the Temple promoted and financed the construction of numerous

RELIGIOUS ORDER OR SECRET SECT?

Some scholars believe that the wisdom of the abbot of Clairvaux was not limited to the theological and philosophical knowledge of the time, but that he was also very well versed in the secrets of Hermetic Christology. In fact, there are those who assert that Bernard was actually a distinguished member of the Priory of Sion, and was one of the "Guardians of the Great Secret," which, according to certain esoteric sources, contained ancestral knowledge and a plan for universal domination. These secrets were passed on to a few initiates from generation to generation, including the Egyptian pharaoh Akhenaton, King David, Jesus, Julian the Apostate, Leonardo da Vinci, Nostradamus, and other historical personages who swam against the current of their times.

The same scholars state that Bernard revealed the ancient secrets he allegedly held to the Templar chiefs, and directed the Order in serving the plan of those ancestral powers. In this version, the Temple was the medieval incarnation of this millenary sect, and not merely a monastic and military brotherhood whose mission was to protect pilgrims—a goal already completely achieved by the Hospitallers of Saint John.

cathedrals, the most famous of which is Chartres. This cathedral was built in 1194 at the former site of some pagan sanctuaries and a sort of druidic seminary. In modern times, it has been verified that certain subterranean currents and tectonic faults meet at this site, producing curious vibrations. The rational explanation resorts to the known interest of the Templars in all types of knowledge, and to the fact that the Order counted among its members scholars and experts in various sciences who were able to detect these exceptional phenomena. The more esoteric interpretations assert that the druids and pagan priests were also "guardians of the Great Secret," and that they handed down knowledge to their successors of the magical location where two altars had stood, connecting with the superior forces of the universe.

Chartres is the cathedral that offers the least doubt with respect to its Templar origin; on the floor of the principal nave there is still a labyrinth showing symbols of the Temple, which are also found in many details of the interior decoration. Novel elements were employed in its construction, such as polyhedral forms, the perfection of the ogival arch, and the use of the golden ratio, which official history attributes to an evolution of the later Roman style, whereas occultist scholars refer to the

Druid, from an illustration in Old England *by Charles Knight, published in England in 1845.*

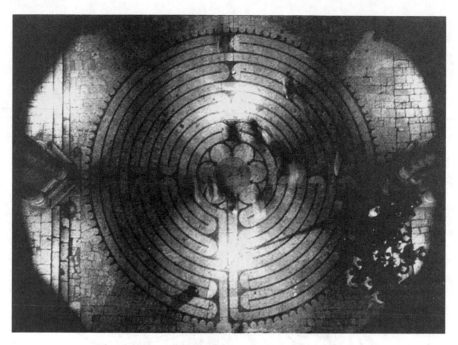

The labyrinth in Chartres Cathedral.

techniques employed for the Egyptian architecture of the Great Pyramid, preserved and handed down by the Phoenician quarrymen who worked on this monumental and enigmatic edifice.

Persecution and Dispersion of the Order

The enormous monies lent to various European monarchs gave the Order of the Temple the opportunity to place discreet advisers in royal courts, who occasionally went beyond giving advice and imposed their views upon the political, military, or commercial actions of the kingdoms in question. Some kings admired and respected the Templars, among them Steven of England, who facilitated their entrance into his kingdom and into Scotland (which ended up being vital to the survival of the Order in perilous times), and Alfonso of Aragon, an heirless king who left his entire kingdom to the Templars in his will. When he died in 1133, the Templars, perhaps so as not to provoke the Muslims by taking over the position of a king who had fought almost thirty battles with them,

Templar knight on his horse, with war habit.

decided to renounce this inheritance in exchange for a large sum offered by the nobles of Aragon.

Other sovereigns, more submissive to pontifical powers even though they asked for and received vital Templar loans—or maybe because of this—conspired among themselves and with the ecclesiastical hierarchies to undermine the immense power that the Order had gained. The most resentful of all of them was King Philip IV of France (Philip the Fair), who was deeply indebted to the Templars. The Templars were also flaunting their power right under the nose of this sovereign, occupying an autonomous, closed-off enclave in his capital, where they had built a fortress and other buildings for the Order's headquarters. Philip knew he could not defeat the Temple without the aid of an unchallenged authority. He therefore appealed to Pope Clement V, who also held a grudge against the Order, and they agreed to act at the same time, by surprise.

One night, in the winter of 1307, the henchmen of Philip the Fair arrested the principal Templar chiefs and all the members of the Order whom they could catch off guard. On the following day, the Vatican ordered the bishops and abbots, as well as the kings and princes obedient to the papacy, to seize all the goods of the Temple and to arrest, without ceremony, all Templar knights who could be found in their respective dominions.

Pope Clement V officially dissolved the Order of the Temple and excommunicated all the masters and knights, handing over their positions and prerogatives to the Hospitallers of Saint John, who already functioned as a sort of personal army for the pope. In compliance with this decree, the High Tribunal of the Inquisition persecuted, incarcerated, and condemned the Templars on the grave charges of "heresy, perjury, sodomy, and Satanism." Many of them, subjected to terrible tortures, confessed to the most absurd crimes, or else died in torment. Others were shut in dungeons for life or sold as slaves, while the Holy See, France, and other kingdoms and dioceses took possession of the castles, fiefdoms, and goods of the Order. But although the papists searched in every corner of Europe, they could not find the fabulous fortune that, according to rumors, the Templars possessed. The last Grand Master, Jacques de Molay, remained a fugitive for four years, until he was caught by the Holy Office, tortured with brutal sadism, and finally burned at the stake. From the point of view of his

Medieval drawing of a Templar knight.

The arrival of the crusaders in Constantinople. (Painting by Gustave Doré.)

vicious adversaries and the enthralled common people, his death marked the definitive end of the Order of the Temple.

However, not all the Templars were caught. In France, many of them hid under the protection of the guild of stoneworkers *(maçons)*, with whom they had formed close bonds in the construction of cathedrals; in Spain they infiltrated other orders, religious and military; and in Germany they incorporated themselves into the Teutonic Knights of the Hanseatic League. But their most surprising trick was the disappearance of the imposing Templar fleet of La Rochelle, which vanished on the same night that Philip the Fair carried out his spiteful raid on the Templar knights.

The Lost Fleet of La Rochelle

The number and type of ships that made up the Templar fleet are not precisely known, but all sources agree in describing it as "large" and "powerful." There is also no information explaining how these ships could have disappeared in such a sudden and opportune manner. The most believable version suggests that the chiefs of the Temple were warned of the danger by their spies in the French court and the Vatican, and thus had a few hours, or even a day or two, to prepare the fleet's escape. This would explain how the ships were prepared, supplied with provisions, and made ready to set sail with full crews and, without doubt, a large cargo of fugitive Templars. Some sources hold that de Molay himself embarked that night, and that his capture four years later occurred while he was returning to accomplish a secret mission.

Many authors write that the great fleet was divided into two or more flotillas, which took different routes in order to disorient their pursuers. Some of the ships headed for Portugal, some for Scotland, and a third squadron probably sailed to the Mediterranean to take refuge in Sicily.

Being relatively near to La Rochelle, Portugal was a destination that permitted the Templar ships to get away from the open sea quickly and hide in coastal inlets, thus avoiding being seen by the papal vessels. In addition, the court of Portugal, unlike those of Spain and France, had traditionally maintained good relations with the Order. Under the protection of King Alfonso IV, the Templars founded an alternative brotherhood, called the

Order of the Knights of Christ, whose first Grand Master was the king himself. Later on, Prince Henry the Navigator was also Grand Master of the clandestine structure maintained by the Order of the Temple.

It is known that Prince Henry was the main instigator of the first voyages and discoveries accomplished by Portuguese mariners such as Vasco da Gama and Pedro Álvarez Cabral to the coasts and islands of West Africa. The apparent purpose of these expeditions was to find a maritime route to the Indies that would avoid the Muslim threat existing along the land routes. However, it is probable that Henry, as secret Grand Master of the Temple, was familiar with the ancient Phoenician and Arabic maps that showed a vast, empty continent to the west of the Azores islands. His plan may have been to test his ships and train his captains on long voyages along the coast of Africa before launching a great transatlantic expedition in search of the lost continent. In fact, as we shall see later, Columbus devised a similar project after his contact with the Templars in Portugal and the Azores.

The remaining Templar ships sailed for Great Britain in order to reach the safe ports of Ireland. From there, they made contact with the separatist Scottish leader, Robert the Bruce, who was at war with England and the Anglophile clans. Robert already ruled a considerable part of Scotland where neither the papal bulls nor the authority of the Vatican, which had recently excommunicated him for his rebellion, was valid. He generously received the Templars, who for their part offered him their collaboration in the campaign against England and its local allies.

The chronicles tell us that on June 24, 1314, Robert went into battle with six thousand men against an army of twenty thousand English soldiers in the decisive Battle of Bannockburn. The spirit and bravery of the rebels were not sufficient to overcome the difference in numbers between the two forces, and the luck of the battle was inclining toward the English. But then, a formation of cavalry bearing its own flags and standards appeared from behind the Scottish rear guard and entered into combat. When the English recognized the Templar emblems and saw the eight-pointed crimson cross on the knights' chests, they were terrified. They scattered, yielding the victory to Robert the Bruce.

With the defeat of the English, Scotland became an independent kingdom without any obligation to the papacy. The Order of the Temple easily installed itself and acquired a number of properties and fiefdoms, especially in the region extending north from Glasgow. The Templars prospered under the protection of the clan of the Saint Clair, or Sinclair, lords of Roslin, a high lineage of Danish origin related by marriage to William the Conqueror and the Stewards (or Stuarts). This last family, to which Robert the Bruce's wife belonged, became rulers of Scotland in 1371 and reigned over England from 1603 to 1714.

The Templars had fought at Bannockburn under the command of Henry Sinclair, whom Bruce made prince of Rosslyn and the Orkney Islands. According to some sources, Sinclair possessed maps made by ancient Phoenician and Arab cartographers indicating the existence of an unknown land on the western side of the Atlantic. The Scottish Grand Master decided to put his efforts into reaching this land—possibly the origin of the legend of Atlantis—and organized a great westward maritime expedition. The other part of his fleet left with no fixed destination, probably to raid Catholic ships on the high seas.

The west entrance to Rosslyn Chapel, surmounted by a magnificent rose window with an "engrailed" cross.

The ships of La Rochelle that arrived in Sicily doubtless found a secure refuge. In the mid-eleventh century, Viking invaders had conquered the south of Italy and defeated the Byzantines and Arabs who were occupying the region. They then established a Norman kingdom whose first monarch was the Scandinavian Templar Roger de Guiscard. At the beginning of the next century, his successor, Roger II, extended his conquests and established an elegant and cultured court in Palermo, adopting the title of king of Sicily. Roger II was a generous and merry sovereign, loving both the arts and the pleasures of life. His subjects called him *le joyeux Roger* (Roger the Jolly). Under his reign the armies and ships of Sicily hoisted one of the standards of the Temple—a skull above two crossed tibias on a black background, which the English referred to as the "Jolly Roger"—which can be seen today on the bas-reliefs of some Templar tombs in Scotland.

When Templar ships arrived in Sicily a century later, fleeing from the papist kingdoms, they adopted the Jolly Roger as their ensign. Soon afterward, the sinister black flag flew from all the Templar ships as the symbol of their war against the Vatican.

PART 2
THE GOLDEN AGE OF PIRACY

3

THE TEMPLE AND
THE PIRATES

In turning to piracy, the Templars not only sought to increase their already considerable resources and seize new ships for their fleets; their underlying and final objective was to destroy the power of the Vatican, attacking the ships of nations that paid allegiance to the papacy and strengthened the hegemony of the Holy See. To this end, Templars operating from Scotland and England sought the complicity of the Norman pirates who were continuing their activities, while those who were settled in Sicily alternated between alliances and battles with the Berber pirates based on the African coast.

Pirates in the Mediterranean

The Spanish coast, across from the African Maghreb, suffered attacks from Saracen pirates for centuries, resulting in a series of defensive measures and military constructions all along Spain's Mediterranean coast, and giving rise to the popular Spanish expression "There are Moors on the coast," referring to an unwanted or inconvenient presence. It is also known that in the fourteenth and fifteenth centuries, Andalusian, Valencian, and Castilian pirates fought in Mediterranean waters with Genovese and Provençal corsairs *a furto* (for stolen goods or booty), while at the same time battling with Moorish pirates. Similar activity, together with trading and smuggling, was undertaken by Portuguese pirates from their base at the African port of Ceuta, opposite Gibraltar. To complete the scene, Navarrese, Mallorcan, and Sardinian pirates also sailed these waters, not to mention the ubiquitous Saracens. Ethnicity and religion were not highly important in the crews; Saracen prisoners often signed up on European ships, and the ships of Muslim kingdoms took on Christian mercenaries. A striking case of this kind of crossover is that of the Catalan pirate Bartomeu Perpinyá, who hindered Valencian maritime commerce in the second half of the fifteenth century, employed by the Muslim king of Granada.

The objective of Spanish pirates after the discovery of America, although they were not above stealing cargoes of supplies, arms, and Eastern mercantile riches, was fundamentally the capture of slaves, whether Muslim or from foreign Christian vessels or ports. With this motive, sea battles were generally fought over access to coastal settlements; the rival seafarers took prisoners from among the people of the villages and hamlets or the farmers and shepherds of the surrounding countryside, and then sold them into the slave trade. The relative stagnation of the Reconquest of Spain from the Moors, the failure of the Crusades, and the fatal effects of the Black Death had reduced the availability of cheap work, or slave labor, for the many chores that were too rough or daunting to be undertaken by the middle class or their nobles.

Supplying foreign slaves to the kingdoms of the Iberian Peninsula became an excellent business, and resulted in a flourishing new coastal and seafaring bourgeoisie in cities such as Barcelona and Seville. Among the prominent Catalan pirates were the famous Roger de Llúria, who harassed the ships of the duke of Anjou, persistent enemy of the counts of Barcelona; Conrad de Llançà, who successfully invaded the Berber ports; and Guillem de Castellnou, who accomplished the annexation of Alicante to the kingdom of Aragon. Here we must also mention the Valencian pirate Jaume Vilarogut, who gained terrible fame for his atrocities. His family acquired great fortune and prestige, to the point that in the fifteenth century, the Vilarogut clan led the Catalan faction that aided the count of Urgell, battling the Centelles family, on the side of Ferdinand of Antequera.

Good examples of Andalusian pirates were the brothers Martín

Alonso and Vicente Yánez Pinzón, from the town of Palos de Moguer near the mouth of the Tinto River in the province of Huelva, who practiced piracy along the coasts of Catalonia. Martín also reached the English Channel in his voyages, as well as the Azores, where he may have known Christopher Columbus, who moved in more or less the same circles. One of these two men may have been a Templar, initiating the other into the secrets of the Order, or perhaps they both belonged to it and their meeting was planned. What is certain is that later on, both brothers participated in Columbus's first expedition, which according to some sources was a punishment imposed by the Catholic monarchs Ferdinand and Isabella for his crimes; according to others, the clandestine Order entrusted the three men with the task of "discovering" America, a subject that will be discussed in more detail later.

At the end of the fifteenth century, the Catholic monarchs decided to prohibit corsair expeditions under their flags. The absolute obedience of Ferdinand and Isabella to the Holy See is well known. For this reason it will not seem strange that they made this decision in response to the papal desire to eliminate piracy, an activity strongly influenced, if not directly committed, by the clandestine organization of the Temple. In any case, the prohibition of privateering resulted in the complete takeover of the Mediterranean by Berber pirates in the service of the Ottoman Empire.

The Turkish pirate of Greek origin Jair al-Din (whom the Italians called Barbarossa because of his bristly red beard), together with his brother Arud, was the initiator of large-scale piracy in the service of the powerful sultan Suleiman the Magnificent. The Barbarossa brothers had the clever idea of recruiting small-time Muslim pirates who were acting independently along the coasts of the Maghreb, as well as numerous European ex-corsairs who were out of work as a result of the edict of the Catholic monarchs, to form a great pirate fleet that would practice privateering under the flag of the Ottoman Empire. Their first successful action was to expel the Spanish from their enclave on the Algerian island of Penon, for which Jair was rewarded by being appointed pasha of Algiers. He immediately expanded and reformed the Algerian port, which became a center and a refuge for the pirates of the Maghreb in the Mediterranean, commonly known as Berbers or Saracens. Jair himself maintained a flourishing regime in Algiers by means of a large and powerful fleet, which undertook fierce battles and occasional alliances with the Templar pirates of Sicily. The Turkish sultans' protection of piracy went so far that in 1534 Redbeard was made high admiral of the Ottoman Empire, at the front of a powerful navy with which he completed the conquest of Tunis.

Meanwhile, Suleiman advanced by land across Europe, seizing Belgrade, defeating Louis II of Hungary, and marching on to Vienna on the banks of the Danube in 1529. The troops of Emperor Charles V (Charles I of Spain) managed to drive back this invasion, saving the Austrian capital from falling into Ottoman hands. But Suleiman's retreat was not the end of his terrorizing of Europe, much less that of the absolute reign over the Mediterranean by the pirate-turned-admiral Barbarossa.

The Thwarted Revenge of the Temple

Some claim the existence of a kind of alliance between Suleiman and the Templars, citing as an argument the great attack on the island of Malta by the Turkish fleet in 1565, involving two hundred warships and five hundred skilled soldiers commanded by Admiral Dragut, successor to Jair al-Din. It is known that the ancient Order of the Hospitaller Knights of Jerusalem, traditional enemies of the Temple, had taken refuge on this island after the failure of the crusades, calling itself the Sovereign Order of Malta. It is possible that the Templars, after three centuries, wanted to avenge themselves on the Hospitallers for their Vatican plotting and encouraged Suleiman to raze the island that served as their enclave. But to the surprise of the Turks, the Maltese were able to repel them under the leadership of Grand Master La Valette.

Another hard blow for the Turks was their defeat at the battle of Lepanto on October 7, 1571. In the Gulf of Corinth in Greece, 280 ships of the Holy League formed by Spain fought three hundred Ottoman vessels. The allied fleet prevailed over its adversaries in a bloody naval battle of boardings and hand-to-hand combat (in which don Miguel de Cervantes lost an arm). Heartened by this triumph, Philip II recommended to his half brother, John of Austria, that he attack the pirate strongholds of North Africa. The "Great Captain" took the city of Tunis and the important fort of La Goleta in 1575, but shortly afterward the Turks captured both places and went back to fighting for supremacy in the Mediterranean.

Moors on the Coast

Since ancient times, the Spaniards have applied the name Moors to all types of pirates, whether they were actually Saracens or from other areas such as Sicily and the Byzantine ports. The people of the Spanish Mediterranean coast were practically defenseless against the Moors' attacks; it was rare for the few ships of the Kingdom of Spain to fight these invaders, and the coastal settlements received only occasional protection from domestic seafarers, who also practiced piracy. To protect themselves from the attacks, the coastal populations took the precautionary action of retreating from the coast and settling inland, choosing elevated areas where possible, such as the towns in the Catalan county of Maresme whose names still have the suffixes *"de mar"* (of the sea) and *"de dalt"* (above). But the danger still persisted, because the fishermen had to go down and launch their boats to practice their trade, and in any case, the pirates did not hesitate to cross the small expanse of land that separated them from their victims. It was thus necessary to build watchtowers to spot pirate ships in time to send for help, prepare defenses, or in many cases simply escape inland carrying only a few prized possessions.

The first watchtowers were built when the Catholic monarchs prohibited the activities of Spanish corsairs, leaving the field wide open for Muslim piracy. The first watchtowers were primitive structures made of planks or tree trunks with space for a single watchman, built on promontories or islands that gave a good view of pirate ships on the horizon. With the growth of French and English piracy beginning in the sixteenth century, the Spanish fleet moved almost completely to the Atlantic and the Caribbean in order to protect the galleons transporting the riches of America. This new activity entirely removed the presence of the Spanish navy along the Iberian coasts, which were now more defenseless than ever.

The building of coastal defenses intensified during the sixteenth century, with more solid towers, esplanades where cannons were placed, and walls with battlements, such as those protecting Málaga, Almería, and Cádiz. In the more exposed cities, great castles were built or fortified, including practically impregnable fortresses such as that of Montjuic in Barcelona and those of Cartagena, Peñíscola, and Cullera.

Another defensive measure was the formation of integrated militias from among the inhabitants themselves, first in a spontaneous manner and later organized as paramilitary forces by the governments and town councils. The distinct bodies of *de custodia* militiamen moved with remarkable rapidity from one point to the next, aiding each other in response to the warnings of danger announced by the watchmen. Whatever the degree of their efficacy, these local troops were the only force available to defend the coastal populations for most of the sixteenth century.

Nevertheless, the "Moors" remained a latent threat to the Spanish coasts, continually striking new blows. Berber piracy continued in the Mediterranean during the following centuries, and finally disappeared only with the French conquest of Algeria in 1830.

American Booty

After the expeditions of Christopher Columbus, the conquest of the so-called West Indies offered Spain undreamed-of riches from mines full of gold, silver, and precious stones. But in order to enjoy this fabulous treasure, it was necessary to travel across the Atlantic, a long and risky voyage. The small and light expeditionary caravels, with lateen sails and no mast tops, were replaced by large, heavy cargo galleons measuring up to thirty meters (a hundred feet) in length, with three to five masts. Their holds, full of precious cargo, presented an irresistible temptation to pirates and were the object and cause of the greatest and most prolonged peak in the long history of maritime banditry.

Independent pirates proliferated in the first decades of the sixteenth century, operating in the Mediterranean and the Atlantic waters off the European coasts, attracted by booty transported in ships that were easy to intercept and board. The majority of pirates did not have ships capable of sailing far out into the Atlantic, and they preferred to lie in wait for their prey on the outskirts of the Canary Islands and the Azores, which were intersection points for merchant ships coming from the East Indies around the African continent, carrying valuable cargoes of Oriental silk and spices. Many of these pirates were French sailors who set up a base on the Canary island of Lobos. In 1556, the French corsair Le Clerc, known as Jambe de Bois (Wooden Leg), attacked and sacked the port of Santa Cruz de la Palma. Although island-based piracy continued for the next two centuries, the vigilance of imperial ships reduced this activity, which was hindered all the more by the rise of pirates on the Caribbean, who gained the upper hand by seizing the richest spoils close to their ports of origin.

The reign of Philip II, who acceded to the throne of Spain in 1556, was not a happy one in terms of combating piracy and protecting American treasure from the corsairs of the Caribbean. A reserved and obsessively Catholic monarch, he managed to deal a hard blow to the Muslims at the battle of Lepanto, but made an enemy of France under Henry of Bourbon, the Huguenot heir-presumptive (and possibly a Cathar and Templar). Furthermore, Spain's neglect of its possessions in Flanders provoked the rebellion of the Low Countries in 1568, which the duke of Alba attempted to quell, with little success. Nor was the king of Spain on good terms with England, which had just broken away from the Holy See, forming its own church and offering protection to Protestants.

In 1568, England and France decided to take the side of the Flemish rebels against Spain. The hostility between the two sides erupted into open war ten years later, when Philip also occupied the vacant throne of Portugal. With this double kingdom, the monarchy obtained complete dominance over the riches of the New World, since a bull of Pope Alexander VI in 1493 had divided the recently discovered continent between Spain and Portugal, a division adjusted a year later at the Treaty of Tordesillas, between the Catholic monarchs and King John II of Portugal. The other European kingdoms therefore could not conquer and settle American territories without defying the Holy See and provoking a conflict in Europe of unimaginable proportions. Under these conditions, with Philip flaunting the two crowns of the Iberian Peninsula and having all the lands and treasures of America at his exclusive disposal, it can be understood that France and England were disconcerted by such a powerful army and so much unjust privilege.

According to official history, these were the reasons, proved and documented beyond doubt, for which France, England, and the recently formed United Provinces (the Netherlands) all rose up against Philip and actively promoted the actions of corsairs in the Caribbean, thus lightening the heavy coffers of the Spanish galleons for their own benefit. But revisionist scholars see the long shadow of the Temple and Freemasonry behind these motives. The Order of the Temple had deep roots in France and the British Isles. In France, the Templars were reestablished, thanks to their links with Huguenots such as King Henry IV of Bourbon. Although he embraced Catholicism solely in order to be allowed to accede to the throne ("Paris is worth a mass," he supposedly said upon converting), the Templars were able to continue in secret during his almost fifty-year reign. In Great Britain, and particularly in Scotland, the presence and influence of the Temple has been recognized since at least the thirteenth century, and it is said that Templar advisers encouraged the temperamental king Henry VIII to break ties with the Vatican and start his own church. Nor is it any coincidence that the northern part of the Low Countries, which formed the United Provinces, was entirely Calvinist; some sources say that Calvin was a Templar who infiltrated the Church in order to support Luther's reform, making it more extensive and entirely removing any potential for agreement with the Holy See.

It should not be forgotten that the Templars knew of the existence of a terra incognita, and had very probably reached its shores. This gave rise to the millenary project of creating a new society in the New World under a more just and spiritual order, removed and liberated from what they considered the Vatican's pernicious domination. In this plan, they had used a member of their order, Columbus, to "officialize" the existence of the unknown continent under the indisputable banner of the Catholic monarchs; but as is known, an obsessively Catholic and papist king entered into their project and took possession of their promised land. They then used their connections and influence in other powerful kingdoms and wielded a weapon with which they were especially expert—piracy—against the Spanish Empire.

Looking at these arguments, it is possible to read the history of piracy as another episode in the prolonged secret war between the Templars and the Vatican. Going a step further, one can see that a good part of European and American history is stained with blood from this war.

The French Buccaneers

King Francis I of France, a frustrated aspirant to the imperial crown obtained by Charles V, maintained a ferocious animosity against the latter—personal as much as political and economic. The two men were the same age and had ascended their respective thrones a few months apart, between 1515 and 1516. When Charles V of Spain also became Emperor Charles V of Germany three years later, Francis dedicated all his forces to destroying the empire that he had been unable to obtain. In 1521, off the coast of the Azores, the pirate Jean Florin (known as El Florentino), at the head of an eight-ship fleet, captured the fabulous treasure of Montezuma, which was being transported by Spanish galleons. Throughout Europe, it was known that France had financed Florin's expedition, and that the French monarch had received part of the rich spoils.

Willing to extend this clever business, France baited the imperial armies by attacking Flanders and starting a war in Italy over the possessions of the Habsburgs. Meanwhile, French pirates crossed the Atlantic, taking a relatively safe route westward from the Canary Islands and entering the Caribbean through the arc of the Lesser Antilles. The return to Europe, for both the Spanish vessels and the pirates, involved passing through the Strait of Florida, which was the object of bitter battles between Spain and France. Along this route, the pirates discovered that the West Indies were not only paradisal islands, but also a well-protected refuge, close to the rich and defenseless Spanish ports of the Caribbean and the ships that sailed from them, weighed down with gold and precious stones. This sea thus became a breeding ground for pirates of every type, much patronized by French financiers and by the Crown itself. Their base of operations and place for resting and supplying was the Haitian island of Tortuga, where the pirates were called buccaneers, or *boucaners,* because of their method of preparing the roast meat that was their principal sustenance.

Charles V thoroughly defeated the French armies in Italy and took Francis I prisoner at Pavia in 1525. Francis renounced his Italian aspirations in 1529 at the Treaty of Cambrai, but his rancor was not appeased by this disappointment. Resigned to the fact that land war was not his forte, he decided to tackle his enemy at sea, attacking the ports and ships that distributed the great wealth obtained in America. According to his cunning strategy, once he had cut off this vital supply line, it would be time to return to the dispute with Charles V over the territories of Europe.

Francis armed and financed every buccaneer who wanted to practice piracy in the name of France, and invested large quantities of money in improving their ships and strengthening the pirate colonies of Tortuga and the other islands of the Caribbean. For his part, Charles V armed his own pirates to attack French merchants on the European coasts, and executed the buccaneer precursor Jean Florin, who had been captured and handed over by the Basque pirate Martín de Irízar. But it was the French corsairs (or those of other nationalities sailing under the French flag) who thrived in this half of the sixteenth century, especially in the waters of the Caribbean.

The vulnerability of Spanish ports in America made them a complimentary bonus to pirate boardings at sea. By 1528, the buccaneers had already sacked and burned the port of San Germán in Puerto Rico, and shortly afterward they tried their luck with larger settlements such as Havana, Santiago de Cuba, Veracruz, and Santa Marta on the Colombian coast. The aristocratic French Freemason Jean-François de la Roque, Count of Roberval, armed his own fleet to cross the Atlantic and sack Santa Maria and Cartagena between 1543 and 1544. The inhabitants of the Spanish settlements offered barely any resistance, and later fled toward the interior carrying their valuables in the same manner, as had their ancestors on the Mediterranean coast. However, the booty obtained was scant, and hardly sufficed to compensate for the enormous costs of the expeditions.

The buccaneers did not dare to pursue the people inland, leaving their ships and supplies unprotected. Nor was there much for them to take from the suddenly vacated villages, since at that time the true riches were being transported directly from the mines to the cargo galleons,

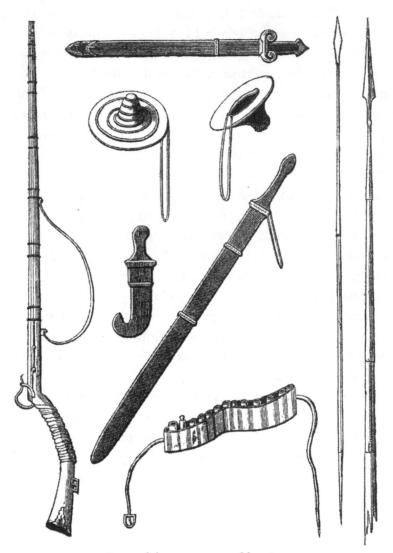

Some of the weapons used by pirates.

which sailed immediately for Spain. The legendary treasures stolen by the French corsairs in their boardings in the waters of the Caribbean were not, in reality, so fabulous. It is estimated that in the four decades between 1520 and 1560, about four thousand ships crossed the Atlantic from America, of which only two hundred were attacked by corsairs; they were not necessarily the richest boats, nor were the corsairs always successful. However, France continued supporting buccaneers such as the previously mentioned "Wooden Leg" Le Clerc, Jean de Bontemps, Jacques Sorel, and Robert Blondel, who terrorized the colonial populations with their violence.

When silver was discovered in Potosi in 1545 (yielding the world's richest mine) and in Mexico a few years later, Charles V resolved to keep his treasures out of reach of the opportunist buccaneers. To this end, he ordered the cargo galleons to be armed with artillery and to sail in convoys of no fewer than ten ships. For their protection, he also ordered a special fleet of warships, armed to the teeth, constituting the *"Armada de la Guardia de la Carrera de las Indias"* (Fleet of the Guard of the Route of the Indies). These ships not only protected the Route of the Indies, but they also transported substantial amounts of silver in their own holds: a very safe location but prohibited by the authorities. This cargo entered Europe as contraband and made the fortune of many captains of the fleet. Among them was the famous Pedro Menéndez de Avilés, who accumulated immense personal wealth from his position as commander of the armada. Despite such shenanigans, the effectiveness of the naval apparatus deployed by Spain to protect its galleons was considerable. To its war power was added the fact that all its force was concentrated on only two great crossings each year, their date of departure guarded in absolute secrecy. The disconcerted buccaneers spent long months at their ports awaiting the passage of a prize that they would not dare to attack once they actually saw it.

Huguenots and Templars

The French Catholics used the term "Huguenots" to refer contemptuously to the Protestants living principally in the south of the country, the center of the Cathar tradition and, according to Christian esotericism, the hiding place of the Holy Grail and cradle of the Merovingian lineage, descended from Jesus of Nazareth. We have already mentioned the almost certain secret antipapist alliance between the thirteenth-century Cathars and the Order of the Temple—then at the height of its power—as well as the Templars' later infiltration of Calvinism. For these reasons it is very probable that, as various scholars state, the clandestine Temple maintained an influence over the Protestants of the region. Amid the wars between the two religions, which dominated the sixteenth century, the Vatican initiated the Counter-Reformation, in which its allied kingdoms persecuted, captured, exiled, and even massacred the Huguenots.

Around 1550, the Huguenot expatriates and fugitives began to seek refuge in America and participate in piracy in the Caribbean. From then on, many buccaneer captains were Protestants (and Templars?), at a time when they were taking control of Tortuga and other pirate colonies.

It was also the Huguenot buccaneers who started and organized the Brotherhood of the Coast in Tortuga, an unusual libertarian society whose rules went beyond the legislation of any kingdom of the time. Its guidelines had little in common with the severe asceticism of Calvinism, and appeared more derived from the higher utopian ideals of the Order of the Temple. Some of its rules were:

- Any prejudice of race, nationality, or religion is strictly prohibited.
- The island belongs to all members equally, and no one may hold individual property on it.
- The Brotherhood may not interfere with anyone's personal freedom, but on the contrary must respect and defend that freedom under all circumstances.
- Nobody is obliged to participate in a pirate expedition if he does not wish to do so.
- Every brother is free to leave the Brotherhood of the Coast at any time.

Another custom of the members of the Brotherhood that recalls the knights of the Temple was that of pairing up with a companion before entering into combat. If one died, the other was considered his "heir." The Brotherhood also established rules for dividing up booty according to the merit of each one in obtaining it, and a table of compensations in coin for those wounded or mutilated in combat.

An equally curious result was that the Huguenot pirates undertook the capture of Florida from the Spanish, doubtless due to the strategic importance of the strait, through which oceanic crossings had to pass, but perhaps also in order to oust the greatest Catholic kingdom from the territory where the Temple planned to build the New Jerusalem. Under the patronage of the Huguenot marshal Gaspar de Coligny, the buccaneers Jean Ribault and René de Laudonnière conquered Florida in 1562 and set up French Protestant colonies there, building the fortified enclave of Fort Caroline (near present-day Jacksonville). From then on, they controlled the passage of the Bahamas and menaced Spanish convoys from a position of strength. The veteran mariner Pedro Menéndez de Avilés, who, as noted earlier, had become rich from smuggling American silver, decided to redeem himself by chartering a squadron to reconquer Florida. In 1565, he set up the fort of Saint Augustine there, and after a series of bloody battles managed to defeat and execute Jean Ribault, recapturing the strategic peninsula for Spain. Menéndez de Avilés was the first governor of Florida, while Coligny, the most prestigious French Huguenot leader, was assassinated in 1572 during the Saint Bartholomew's Day massacre.

Henry II, son and successor of Francis I, dedicated himself to persecuting the Huguenots of France with tremendous cruelty, and withdrew all support from the Protestant buccaneers of the Caribbean. Ready to conquer large areas in other parts of America, he sent two expeditions between 1534 and 1543 to navigate the Saint Lawrence River in Canada, under the command of Jacques Cartier and the pirate count Jean-François de Roberval, whose merciless attack on Cartagena was mentioned earlier. But both attempts to conquer Canadian territories ended in failure, and the French monarch turned his attention back to South America. He then entrusted the cartographer Guillaume le Testu with the task of making a detailed map of the coast of Brazil, where smugglers from Normandy had already long been operating. In 1555, Henry sent the bold and popular adventurer Nicolas de Villegaignon, a soldier, pirate, explorer, and scientist, to South America for the foolish purpose of founding an "Antarctic France" there. With only two ships and about three hundred men, Villegaignon sailed into Guanabara Bay and planted the French flag at the site where Rio de Janeiro would be founded a decade later. But the Portuguese wasted no time expelling the rash Frenchmen from their territory.

Disheartened by these defeats and embroiled in religious wars, France abandoned its American ambitions, at least for the time being.

At the end of the sixteenth century, the buccaneers were near the end of their peak, maintaining only a residual presence in the next epoch, which was dominated by the great corsairs of Elizabethan England.

The Corsairs of the English Empire

Elizabeth I, daughter of Henry VIII and Anne Boleyn, was the great promoter and protector of the famous English pirates who accomplished notable deeds in the last decades of the sixteenth century. These were the precursors of other famous corsairs who harassed and robbed Spanish ships in the following centuries, consolidating English domination of the seas. Their activity weakened the power and wealth of Spain's empire more than anything else, including the defeat of the Spanish Armada in 1588.

The names of these corsairs passed into the history and legend of piracy; they were considered heroes of the sea by the English and accused by the Spanish of being ferocious criminals. We shall continue by briefly recounting the deeds and adventures of a few of the most famous ones.

Elizabeth I, the Virgin Queen, laid the foundations of the British Empire throughout almost half a century of reign. (Anonymous portrait of Elizabeth I, English School of the sixteenth century.)

Francis Drake, the Queen's Corsair

Around 1560, a sagacious English merchant by the name of John Hawkins began a fruitful business of slave smuggling between Africa and the Americas. The Laws of the Indies required slave labor to be supplied only by the slave market administered by the House of Trade in Seville, but the offerings of this monopoly were not sufficient, and the colonists of the New World, unable to harvest their crops, were driven to desperation. This situation was especially grave in the plantations that required many workers for picking, such as coffee, cotton, and tobacco. Their owners were entirely willing to break the law and pay good money for the shipments of smuggled African slaves. Hawkins discovered this, as did certain commercial companies in which the Crown had a share.

Elizabeth I acceded to the throne in 1558, and it remains a controversial question whether she knew she was investing in the slave trade and sponsoring the flagship of the slave trading fleet. For some years, Hawkins made a fortune for himself and his sponsors by smuggling slaves to the New World, where plantation owners clandestinely bought them. Although his activity was civilian, he did not hesitate to fire his guns and cannons whenever some local governor, overly zealous on the side of the law, tried to impede his work. The company of shipowners associated with Hawkins punctually paid a portion of their income to the Crown; perhaps the powerful minister William Cecil concealed this fact from the queen.

In 1567, on his third voyage, Hawkins took his nephew Francis Drake along as a deputy. Despite being not yet thirty years old, the young man was an expert mariner, having sailed the Bay of Biscay and smuggled contraband in America with Captain John Lovel. The expedition with his uncle was unfortunate, since they were surprised by a great storm that dismasted the flagship and set them off course. Hawkins and Drake then sailed for the Honduran port of San Juan de Ulúa, intending to repair the serious damage they had sustained. But cannon fire from the fort prevented their approach, and meanwhile the sails of a Spanish war squadron appeared in the distance. Trapped between a rock and a hard place, the smugglers went into battle in the roadstead of the port. During combat, Drake managed to escape in his ship, the *Swan,* leaving Hawkins to his fate. Upon arrival in

England, Drake said that his uncle had died in combat—but Hawkins appeared safe and sound a few weeks later, accompanied by a few other survivors. It is not known what the uncle and nephew said to each other upon meeting again, but it is known that they returned to sailing together some years later.

Francis Drake then decided to become a pirate in the Caribbean, with results so devastating for Spain that King Philip II offered 20,000 ducats for his head. His first expedition, consisting of the ships *Swan* and *Pasha,* sailed from Portsmouth in 1572. Their destination was the Colombian port of Nombre de Dios, where they captured the rich cargoes of several Spanish vessels. From there they crossed the Isthmus of Panama to gaze upon the Pacific, a view that inspired certain dreams and plans. Upon returning to England, Drake placed himself in the service of the earl of Essex in his struggle with Ireland, attacking the Irish ships and coast at the command of three frigates. Shortly before dying, Essex presented Drake to the queen as the best of his naval captains.

When the earl of Essex presented Drake to her, Elizabeth was thirty-seven: almost old by the standards of the era. He, by contrast, was only thirty—young and quite handsome, with the aura of manliness and bravery that always surrounded sailors, especially pirates. Elizabeth was called the "Virgin Queen" for remaining single, turning down one lofty suitor after another. It is indubitable that there was a significant attraction between Drake and the queen, based upon mutual admiration. According to court gossip, some historians, and many novels and films, the two carried on a passionate and secret love affair. No proof exists of this, but—it must be said—there is no proof that remaining single meant that the queen had to remain a virgin.

At this audience, or at a later one, Drake told the queen of his plan to sail for the South Pacific, with the intent of attacking the defenseless Spanish colonies on the South American coast. Elizabeth gave him five well-armed ships, and in December 1577, Drake set sail directly for Rio de la Plata. From there he went on with two of his ships to skirt Patagonia, where he had some skirmishes with the natives, and finally reached the tortuous strait that Magellan had discovered in 1520. In this passage, he lost his second ship, which actually set off back to England, leaving the flagship *Golden Hind* alone under Drake's command. He then abandoned his plan to attack Panama and decided to sack the ports of Chile and Peru, boarding the merchant ships departing from those places. His great accomplishment was the capture of the vessel *Nuestra Señora de la Concepción,* called the *Caca Fuego* (literally, "Shitfire") for being the most heavily armed ship of the Spanish squadron of the Pacific. The ship transported a rich treasure of gold ingots, silver coins, and chests full of pearls and other jewelry, with a value of £150,000—a fabulous fortune in those days.

Convinced that the Spanish navy would catch him along any of the habitual return routes, Drake conceived the bold idea of returning to Europe across the Pacific, just as Juan Sebastián Elcano had done in his day. He sailed for the coast of Mexico to get supplies, where he hoped to encounter better winds for the voyage, and embarked westward at the end of July 1579. On the journey he drew cartographical outlines of the islands and coasts that he encountered and established cordial relations with various local rulers, laying a very useful basis for the English commercial empire in Asia that would be established a hundred years later.

After a voyage of almost three years, Francis Drake arrived at Plymouth in September 1580, bringing intact the valuable booty from the *Caga Fuego* and other ships he had attacked during his campaign. The queen gave him a warm welcome, perhaps because of her confused feelings for him, and certainly because her corsair had made her immensely rich. Elizabeth went on board the *Golden Hind* and conferred upon Drake the title of knight in a ceremony of pomp and solemnity. Officially, this distinction was not given for being the greatest and most lucrative seafaring thief, but rather for being the first English navigator to circumnavigate the globe, the pioneer cartographer of the South Seas, the valiant captain who had defeated the enemy ships that tried to hinder these achievements—and also, possibly, for being a traveling lover returning triumphant to the arms of the queen.

Francis Drake's career did not end with this extraordinary triumph. In 1585 he set out again for the Caribbean, this time at the head of a fleet of twenty-five ships, with which he took the island of Santo Domingo. Upon his return, triumphant once more, he brought the first samples of tobacco to England, and probably the first potatoes. Two years later, Elizabeth sent him to attack the port of Cádiz, and in 1588

Queen Elizabeth I of England knighting Sir Francis Drake (1540–1596) on board his ship, the Golden Hind, *in Deptford. Drake returned from his successful circumnavigation of the globe in September 1580, bearing numerous treasures taken from the Spanish.*

he commanded, as vice admiral, one of the English squadrons that defeated the "invincible" Spanish Armada. It is said that his action in the Battle of the Channel was brilliant, using pirate tactics such as sending out small boats filled with flaming coal tar toward the hulls of the enemy ships. In following years, promoted by Elizabeth to the rank of admiral, Drake attempted an attack on La Coruña—which was thwarted by the heroic resistance of the Galicians—and carried out other, smaller incursions upon the Spanish coast.

In 1595, Francis Drake went on his last campaign, together with his veteran uncle Hawkins, each in his own flotilla. Both failed in successive attacks on Las Palmas de Gran Canaria and later on the island of Puerto Rico, which got its name ("Rich Port") for obvious reasons. William Hawkins died in combat and his nephew retreated, disappointed and sick with malaria. The illness worsened during the voyage, and the celebrated corsair died near Portobelo on the Panamanian coast. His death caused great rejoicing in Spain, where the churches set their bells to ringing and writers such as Cervantes and Lope de Vega wrote poems celebrating the happy event.

Henry Morgan, the Invincible Pirate

The name Henry Morgan has always been synonymous with corsair; he was without doubt the most famous, bold, and invincible of them all. Born in Wales in 1635 into a respectable military and naval family, he followed this tradition and joined the army. His godfather, the duke of Albemarle, gave him the rank of captain in the English expeditionary squadron that attempted to take the island of Hispaniola from Spain. But the English were weakened by the area's oppressive climate and an epidemic of dysentery, and the Spanish defenders drove them away. The squadron then headed for Jamaica, where Morgan joined the brave commodore Sir Christopher Mings in a voyage of piracy through the Caribbean in 1659. On this profitable journey, they attacked Cumaná and Puerto Cabello in Venezuela and other Spanish enclaves, obtaining impressive spoils amounting to twenty-two coffers of silver coins.

With his part of the winnings, Henry Morgan was able to charter his own ship, with which he accompanied Mings on new excursions. In 1660 they attacked Santiago de Cuba and sacked it in a week, setting fire to the fortifications before leaving. The two successful comrades continued to sail together until 1662, the year in which the commodore was summoned by the Admiralty to join the fleet that was fighting in Holland. Morgan took command, taking over the corsair's patent that had been conceded to Mings, and had his rough initiation as a pirate in 1663. He received information on the rich and unprotected Mexican city of San Juan de Villahermosa, never yet attacked by pirates because of its distance from the sea. Morgan and his men set sail for Villahermosa, sacking it without encountering any resistance. Upon returning with their booty, they found that a Spanish flotilla had discovered their ships and burned them after killing their sentinels. The pirate, indignant at this trick, went on to steal four ships from another nearby port, and with them attacked Gran Granada in broad daylight, increasing his already substantial spoils.

In 1667, Henry Morgan was elected admiral of the Brotherhood of the Coast, the ancient society of buccaneers of the island of Tortuga. Shortly afterward, the English governor sent him to intercept a Spanish fleet that was allegedly headed to retake the island of Jamaica. Morgan accepted the official funds but disobeyed orders, heading instead for Hispaniola to attack Port-au-Prince. The booty was not the best, however, because the inhabitants had already been warned and had fled with their goods to the interior of the island. Wanting to make up for this, Morgan sailed to Jamaica and prepared a fleet of twenty-five ships of every type, with which he attacked the Panamanian city of Portobelo in 1668. The pirates were surrounded by Spanish troops, but they resisted the blockade for a month and finally succeeded in escaping with a plentiful treasure in gold and precious stones and a sum of 250,000 pesos (eight million today) paid by the governor to stop him from destroying the city.

Henry Morgan's fame had already reached both sides of the Atlantic, eliciting admiration from the British and hatred from the Spanish. The famous pirate then decided to take a break, taking advantage of a moment of peace between Spain and England. He acquired a plantation of eight hundred fifty acres near the village of Chapelton in Jamaica, where he moved with his family; the place is still known today as Morgan's Valley.

But this comfortable interlude was not to last. Despite the cessation of hostilities, some Spanish corsairs continued marauding throughout the West Indies and menacing its coasts. The Jamaican authorities called upon Morgan in 1670 and made him commander in chief of all the ships stationed on the island. The famous pirate now had at his disposal the greatest corsair fleet that had ever sailed the Caribbean, composed of thirty-eight ships and corvettes, with a total crew of more than two-thousand men. Their mere appearance was sufficient to make the marauders scatter, at which point Morgan decided to level a cautionary attack on Panama. The Spanish governor, Juan Pérez de Gusmán, had prepared a ruse that he considered brilliant and infallible: He had captured two herds of oxen, which he thought would stampede upon the unsuspecting attackers. But when the moment came, the stratagem did not work. According to an authorized historian, "the oxen were only frightened by the pirates, and scattered in retreat, in one of the more comical episodes of military history." Pérez de Gusmán, embarrassed, set fire to the city before abandoning it to retreat.

The humorous episode was much celebrated in Jamaica but caused no amusement in London, where the government was eager not to disrupt its recent peace with Spain. Morgan was arrested for insubordination and sent back to England in 1670. He then spent almost two years in closely guarded freedom, with a high sum paid for bail, waiting for the king to decide his fate. Charles II did not dare condemn the hero of Portobelo and Panama, admired by his subjects as a loyal and valiant patriot. Instead, he decided to knight him and make him governor of Jamaica. The variable interplay of alliances among European powers had changed, and this designation meant entrusting the defense of the island to the best possible commander in the event of an attack from the French navy. But the attack never happened, and Sir Henry Morgan enjoyed his position for more than ten years, until dying of natural causes at his plantation at Chapelton. He was only fifty-two, but the excesses of his pirate days had taken their toll.

William Kidd, the Scourge of the Indies

After participating in various pirate raids on French ships (among them the sinking of the *Marie Galante*), the young mariner whom everyone knew as Captain Kidd landed at the port of New York. In 1691 he had undertaken a marriage of convenience with a rich widow, which allowed him to socialize with the politicians and businessmen of the city. Thus he began a close friendship with a New York businessman named Robert Livingston. The two traveled to London in 1695 to meet with Richard Coote, earl of Bellomont, who had just been made governor of New York and Massachusetts. The three men agreed upon an ingenious plan: to capture pirate ships in the name of the Crown, but keep the booty instead of returning it to its owners. Coote aroused the interest of members of the Admiralty and the Supreme Court, as well as the Secretary of State and probably Queen Mary herself, in this business of indirect piracy, raising a sum of £6,000 to finance the expedition.

Captain Kidd sailed from London in May 1696 with his new ship, the *Adventure*, a three-hundred-ton galley with thirty-four cannons, bound for New York. There he recruited an expert crew, and in September of that year began a voyage around the coast of Africa, bound for the Indian Ocean. On August 15, 1697, he sighted a convoy of Indian vessels escorted by a

A popular depiction of Captain Kidd (1645–1701).

ship from the East India Company, which forced him to retreat prudently. After a skirmish with two Portuguese ships, Kidd landed at the Laccadive Islands for repairs. The pirate crew treated the natives with cruelty, making them work like slaves, raping their women, and using their boats as fuel for their fires.

When Kidd returned to the sea, news of the brutal conduct of his pirates had spread throughout the region. He managed to elude another company ship, despite his artilleryman William Moore's insistence that they attack it, an insistence Moore reiterated when they came upon a Dutch merchant vessel. Fed up with his subordinate's attitude, Kidd cracked Moore's skull with a heavy bucket and had his body thrown overboard. The crew took good note of the example given by their captain, and there was no more insubordination aboard the *Adventure*.

Boardings of merchant ships by pirates usually resulted in a large number of victims.

Captain Kidd's great deed, which has passed into the history of piracy, occurred in January 1698 when he attacked the *Quedah Merchant,* sailing under the auspices of the Indian government. The ship was on its way from Bengal to Surat carrying a rich cargo of gold coins, silk, arms, and spices. Kidd sold part of this treasure for £10,000, and later set his course for the Saint Mary's Islands to share out the rest of the booty with his crew. In this port he stumbled upon his old rival Robert Culliford, who had stolen his ship in the Caribbean eight years earlier. The two pirates were cautious and respectful of one another and, for once, behaved in a knightly manner. Culliford, who was short on crew, hired a good number of Kidd's men. Kidd burned the wrecked *Adventure* and left the Saint Mary's Islands in November 1698 on board the *Quedah Merchant,* now renamed the *Adventure Prize.*

At the time that Kidd stole the *Quedah Merchant* from it, the East India Company had already endured attacks from the pirate Henry Every and faced the fury of the sovereign of India, who threatened to prohibit all European commerce in his seas and territories. Pressured by this threat, the company bribed high Indian officials, paid large compensations to the owners of the merchant ships that Kidd had stolen, and paid to have squadrons pursue him across the seas south of India. But not only did they not succeed in catching him, but the boardings that Kidd and other pirates perpetrated intensified as well. In 1698, the British governor, seeing his lucrative maritime commerce with the Orient seriously threatened, offered a pardon to all pirates willing to cease their activities—except for Captain Kidd. Regarding the latter, he sent out a general order to search all corners of the sea to capture him. The definitive hunt had begun.

Kidd, who had returned to the Caribbean to ask for the protection of the governor of Saint Thomas (a Danish colony at the time), found out that there was an order for his capture and that the Danes would not protect him. In April 1699 he sailed for the Bay of Savona, on the south side of Hispaniola (now Santo Domingo). There he abandoned the *Adventure Prize,* which was too well known to his pursuers, and bought a modest corvette. After stopping without difficulty in New Jersey and Long Island, he went to Boston, seeking the aid of his old partner, Governor Coote. To his surprise, Coote ordered his arrest, perhaps in order to gain merit and stay clear of the political scandal unfurling in London, where the two principal parties were accusing each other of profiting from Kidd's booty. The prisoner was taken the next year to England, where his judges were quick to declare him guilty of piracy; and since this was not enough reason to hang him, they also found him guilty of killing the aggressive artilleryman William Moore. The sentence was carried out on May 23, 1701, with the disagreeable incident of the first rope breaking, so he had to be hanged twice. Captain Kidd's corpse, chained up and covered with tar, was displayed publicly as an example at Tilbury Point, on the outskirts of London. The remains of the famous pirate were left hanging there, in full view of all sailors, until they had rotted away.

The Terrible Edward Teach, or "Blackbeard"

The chronicles say that the pirate Blackbeard terrified his enemies by going into combat with smoldering hemp wicks woven into the curls of his beard. At the same time, the pistols he held at his belt would fire without ceasing while he roared and cursed like the devil himself. He combined this fearsome appearance with an aggressive character and a violent, harsh, and successful disposition. His origin and ancestry remain practically unknown. Although he said that his name was Edward Teach and that he came directly from hell, some experts believe that his true name was Drummond and that he was born into a well-to-do family in Bristol, receiving enough education to read and write fluently. This has not been confirmed, and those who knew Blackbeard would doubtless have sworn that it was not true.

Teach appeared on the scene around 1713 as a Royal Navy sailor in Queen Anne's war against the French. Three years later, he was at the command of the *Queen Anne's Revenge,* a Royal Navy ship with forty cannons. It is not known how he acquired this ship or why he joined with the pirate Benjamin Hornigold to practice piracy in the Caribbean and along the coasts of English North America. Edward Teach became famous just as much for his disproportionate liking for rum and women as for his stature (he was well over six feet tall) and his imposing appearance: a thick beard of dark braided curls, a black hat, a black cloak, and six or seven loaded pistols on his bandoleer and belt. With his bellowing and pyrotechnics added to all this, it is no surprise that according to the chronicles, his victims fled in terror before such a frightening spectacle without putting up a fight.

Blackbeard quickly abandoned his partner and continued his career solo. After blockading the Charleston Harbor in 1718, he terrorized the waters all the way from Honduras to Virginia with a flotilla of four ships and a crew of some four hundred pirates. On this voyage he attacked and boarded twenty merchant ships, neither the Spanish nor the English being able to capture him. Shortly afterward, he made a treaty with the governor of North Carolina, persuading him to turn a blind eye while Blackbeard attacked ships in nearby waters. Of course, the governor received a share of the booty obtained.

But the governor of Virginia, who was not as corrupt as his peer, sent out two warships to capture the pirate, who was attacking his coastline. Teach fled with nineteen men in a corvette, and dropped anchor in the salt marshes off Ocracoke Island in North Carolina. The waters to which he escaped were too shallow for the large warships, so the English captain sent two corvettes with sixty armed men to capture the twenty fugitives. A bitter and unequal combat between them

With a smoldering beard, the grim-faced Captain Edward Teach (1680–1718) was the pirate known as Blackbeard who terrorized the coasts of the West Indies, the Carolinas, and Virginia.

ended in slaughter. The English lost ten men and twenty-four others were wounded; Teach's entire crew ended up dead or seriously injured. Blackbeard himself was the last to fall, fighting hand to hand, and he fought back ferociously even after receiving an estimated twenty-five sword and bullet wounds. He finally died when a blow from a sword severed his head.

Bartholomew Roberts, the Fortunate

Bartholomew Roberts, from a well-to-do family with a good name, chose piracy not for economic reasons or to elude justice, but almost by chance. However, he was perhaps the richest and most fortunate pirate of the entire golden age, capturing four hundred batches of booty in only a four-year career. Another distinctive characteristic of Roberts, compared to his peers, was his moderation in drinking and his avoidance of any type of gambling, which he also strictly prohibited among his crew. Despite these puritanical tendencies, he was also the cruelest of all the pirates; his tactic consisted of terrifying people before fighting in order to preserve his life and those of his men.

Born in Wales in 1682, Bartholomew Roberts enlisted in the English Merchant Navy while still very young. He soon achieved the rank of officer. In 1719 he sailed along the west coast of Africa as second-in-command on board the *Rover,* a slave ship that was headed for the East Indies with its human cargo. The *Rover* was attacked and captured by a pirate ship, whose captain was also Welsh. Roberts was fascinated by the impressive attack, and he easily convinced his countryman to let him partner with the pirates. A few weeks later, the pirate captain was killed in action during a boarding, and the crew elected Roberts as their new chief.

Convinced that all this success was a sign of his destiny, Bartholomew Roberts applied himself enthusiastically to piracy. His name spread rapidly throughout the African and American coasts, as did his nickname, Black Bart (an abbreviation of both Bartholomew and the title of baronet), a probable allusion to his aristocratic origin and his dark and implacable cruelty.

Bartholomew Roberts, like other pirates of his time, used the cruelty with which he treated his prisoners as a tactical resource, a kind of tool of his trade. The more cruel and heartless he showed himself to be— humiliating, torturing, and killing captured crews without mercy—the more his terrible fame grew among those whom he would attack in the future. These people preferred to hand over their ships with their possessions rather than fight back and meet the fate of the defeated. In this way, the pirates avoided cannon battles and hand-to-hand combat, the result of which was uncertain and always costly in terms of damage and fallen men. This certainly did not absolve them of their wickedness, least of all when, moved by either professional custom or personal sadism, they massacred every member of the crews they captured, regardless of whether they offered resistance.

A historian of piracy described Bartholomew Roberts as "quick and savage," writing that "he did not hesitate in using torture and killing to reach his goals." A good example of this was an episode that occurred in 1719, when Black Bart boarded an armed British merchant vessel transporting eighty slaves, near the African coast, a place and situation very similar to the episode that had launched him into piracy. The English captain had the imprudence to resist, refusing to hand over the ship and his human cargo. Roberts overcame this resistance with his accustomed speed and efficacy, putting the survivors to the sword and burning the subjugated vessel. The slaves chained up in the hold were not freed, but rather burned to death or jumped into the sea in their chains, only to be eaten by sharks. This criminal decision of Roberts was also a grave error, since had it not been for his cruelty, he could have sold these ill-fated people for a good price.

Black Bart carried on his reign of terror on the American coasts, eventually using a fleet of four ships and five hundred fierce pirates. His flagship was the *Royal Fortune,* a forty-two-cannon frigate stolen from the French. To throw off his pursuers, he frequently changed his post of command, moving from ship to ship or changing the ships' names, so that the *Royal Fortune* could in reality be three or more distinct ships.

Black Bart's most spectacular victory took place in 1721 off the Brazilian coast. Seeing a large Portuguese fleet of forty-two merchant vessels, he boarded a ship that was lagging behind and forced its captain to tell him which ship was carrying the most valuable cargo. The terrified captain indicated a large vessel armed with forty guns. The *Royal Fortune* of the moment took the Portuguese ship by surprise and made a breach in its hull through which the pirates climbed aboard, while Roberts's ship kept the rest of the fleet at bay with broadsides from its cannons. The booty was worth the exploit: an enormous cargo of gold ingots, coins, diamonds, and other precious stones, along with large quantities of highly valuable sugar, furs, and tobacco.

In 1722, the well-known corsair Woodes Rogers was made governor of some of England's possessions in America. The main motive behind this surprising nomination was to entrust to him the elimination of piracy, a subject with which he was very familiar. Rogers decided to begin with Black Bart, and sent out a naval squadron in his pursuit, led by the fifty-cannon frigates *Swallow* and *Weymouth*. Roberts's cunning was no use against the experience of the pirate turned governor, whose ships caught up with him near the Bahamas as he was fleeing out to sea. They then began their pursuit across the Atlantic, and later along the length of the African coast, until in February 1722 Black Bart thought he had escaped them and anchored his ships at Cape Lopez. A few days later, he saw a slow merchant ship and sent out his second vessel, the *Ranger,* to attack it. But the innocent-looking civilian ship turned out to be the armed *Swallow,* which had lowered its flags and slowed down to deceive the pirates. The captain of the *Ranger* realized the trick too late to flee, and presented a valiant resistance for almost two hours, until his ship foundered, destroyed.

The English then attacked the unprepared *Royal Fortune,* still anchored in the roadstead, and this time cannon fire was exchanged for over three hours to quell the fierce resistance of the crew. Three pirates were killed; another ten wounded; and 152 decided to capitulate due to the inferiority of their artillery, which had not killed any of their enemies. Bartholomew Roberts fell into the sea, mortally wounded, giving rise to the legend that he survived and swam to shore and will reappear one day at the command of a new and even more terrible *Royal Fortune.*

"Calico Jack" and the Pirate Women

Jack Rackham was known as Calico Jack because he habitually wore trousers and a jacket made of this thin West Indian cotton fabric. His name would have languished in anonymity as just another pirate among those swarming around the Caribbean, seizing modest spoils now and then and interspersing these minor offenses with requests for clemency from the authorities, had it not been for his relationship with the two most famous pirate women in history.

Calico Jack's criminal career began with his sailing as boatswain of the *Treasure* under the command of the famous freebooter Charles Vane, traditional rival of the pirate governor Woodes Rogers. One day in 1717, the *Treasure* sighted a solitary French merchant vessel that looked like an easy prize, but for some reason Vane refused to attack it. His crew rose up in mutiny at what they thought was their captain's cowardice, and turned over the command of the ship to Rackham, who led the boarding successfully. A few days afterward, the *Treasure* dropped anchor off a desert island to make some repairs and allow its men to take a rest. Here they were surprised by two pirate corvettes from Jamaica and robbed of the booty they had taken.

Jack then sailed for Providence, Rhode Island, where he handed himself over to the authorities and sought the pardon of Governor Rogers. The latter took his time, but finally confirmed the pirate's pardon in May 1719. Meanwhile, Rackham had made friends in Providence with a colleague named James Bonny, secretly flirting with his attractive wife, Anne. She was the illegitimate daughter of an influential Irish lawyer and his maid, who had escaped to America amid the widely publicized scandal surrounding the affair, settling in Charleston, South Carolina. There the young Anne, who was known for being tough and quarrelsome, was married to Bonny, an adventuring seaman who went into small-time piracy soon afterward. Thus they met Rackham, with whom Anne began a passionate affair. When she became pregnant, she escaped her husband's anger by running away with her lover. The two joined a group of unoccupied pirates and stole a corvette, with which Calico Jack started the second stage of his criminal career, this time in much better company.

After stealing the corvette, Calico Jack and Anne sailed for Cuba. There she gave birth to a son at the house of some friends and entrusted him to their care. Anne quickly learned how to handle pistols and machetes, started wearing men's clothing, and went into battle with the best of them. She and Jack sailed around the Caribbean between Haiti and Bermuda, capturing various small and defenseless ships. When they were short on crew, they often incorporated crewmen from the ships they had taken. Among these crewmen, upon one occasion, was a young and attractive sailor named Mark Read, who awakened Anne's interest. It was quickly discovered that the young man was in reality a woman, and that her true name was Mary Read. To the pirates' astonishment, she told her fantastic story to Anne Bonny and Calico Jack.

Anne Bonny was one of the most famous pirate women of the eighteenth century.

Jack offered to let Mary join his crew, an offer she accepted with enthusiasm. She soon established a close friendship with Anne, and they participated in attacks and captures as deputies of Calico Jack. According to some chronicles, they were the real commanders of the ship and directed the operations, fighting side by side with the other pirates. For the next two years, Rackham and his women made various captures, which gained them fame and respect in the ports around the Caribbean and the coasts of the British colonies. In October 1720 they landed in Jamaica to take a break. For the pirates, "taking a break" meant letting off steam in the taverns and brothels, gambling away the booty they had acquired, and getting drunk on rum. Calico Jack and his companions paid honor to this tradition. One night, while they were all passed out from drinking, they were attacked by the English. Only Anne and Mary were even able to stand up; the latter shouted to her weakened companions to take up arms and fight like men.

THE EXTRAORDINARY ADVENTURES OF MARY READ

Mary had been born illegitimate, the fruit of the indiscretion of an English lady. This lady also had a legitimate son who had died suddenly, and so she dressed Mary as a boy to present to her parents in place of the deceased son. In this way, the alleged "Mark" would be able to inherit the family fortune. It is not known whether the trick worked, or whether the inheritance mentioned was large, but what is certain is that Mary, always wearing men's clothing, joined the Royal Navy as a cabin boy and later served in the infantry. While serving in a dragoon regiment in the War of the Spanish Succession, she fell in love with a fellow soldier and they escaped to Holland to get married, opening up a tavern and guesthouse there. Mary, for the first time, tried on women's clothing and feminine hairdos, and led the life of a young wife, but her husband died shortly afterward from a fever. The distraught widow then took up with a Dutch merchant who was sailing for the West Indies. When on the journey Calico Jack and Anne Bonny attacked the ship, Mary quickly threw on some of her companion's clothes and presented herself before them as "Sailor Read."

Mary Read, the other famous woman pirate, reveals her true sex to a surprised sailor after beating him in combat.

Later, they were all tried and condemned to be hanged. The two women were pregnant, probably both by Rackham, and begged to have the sentence postponed until they had given birth. Calico Jack did not escape, and was publicly hanged in Jamaica on November 28. Shortly afterward, Mary died of a fever at age thirty-seven without having given birth. Anne Bonny's fate is not known, since there are no records of her execution. One version claims that she was rescued by her father, who had become a rich merchant, and that she settled with her child in Virginia, where she entered into a happy and suitable marriage.

The Secret Presence of the Temple

What role did the Templars play in this great golden age of piracy? Did they infiltrate the ranks of these cruel and vicious pirates and become their leaders? What motives are attributed to them by those who claim there was a close relationship between the Order of the Temple and the most famous bandits of the sea? The answers to these questions must be sought in the distant past, combining certain mysterious connections with historical accounts, seafaring traditions, chronicles, and recently discovered ancient maps and documents.

Christian esotericism, opportunely resurrected by various authors of recent best sellers, revolves around the recurring theme of a possible marriage between Jesus and Mary Magdalene. After the death of Christ, Joseph of Arimathea allegedly took the young widow, who was pregnant, to the region south of Gaul where the Cathars later emerged, supposedly as followers of the true Christianity that had come from the Holy Land. A few centuries after the suppression of the Cathars, this part of southern France was the gathering place of the Huguenots, whose ties with the Templars have been related. It is said that Mary Magdalene gave birth in

The arrest of Cathars in Carcassonne, from a fourteenth-century illustration.

France to a girl named Sarah, whose descendants constituted a sacred lineage whose members remained in secrecy in their castle in the Languedoc, hiding from the agents of the Vatican who sought to exterminate them.

The lineage of Jesus was joined by marriage to the Merovingian dynasty, which reigned in France between the sixth and eighth centuries. Although their adversaries called them "the long-haired kings," because they refused to cut their hair for reasons of honor (strangely following the Hebrew tradition of Samson), some chroniclers of the time called them the "thaumaturge [miracle-working] kings," stating that a few drops of their blood would cure any illness. The Merovingian monarchs descended into fratricidal quarrels, and a dynasty of Frankish stewards took power behind the throne, becoming the new guardians of the Great Secret. One of them, Charles Martel, held off the Muslim invaders in the best style of Templar chivalry at the battle of Poitiers in 721. His grandson was the great emperor Charlemagne, who made a pact with the pope to unite all of Europe under the Carolingian Empire. It is said that in order to get the pope to crown him, Charlemagne promised to turn over the Great Secret to him, but some mysterious knights, precursors of the Priory of Sion, managed to rescue the Secret and hide it in a new, secure place. This tradition appears to have been mixed later on with the Arthurian chronicles, as the *Saint Grial,* the chalice from the Last Supper sought by Sir Galahad, mutated into *Sang Real,* meaning "royal blood" in French and pronounced similarly (in fact, Galahad was also the name of an ancient region of the Holy Land).

The Order of the Temple, founded in Jerusalem as the military wing of the Priory of Sion, might have been given the mission to protect ancient testimonies to Jesus' fatherhood, as well as certain God-given knowledge and sacred relics of great spiritual and material value that the knights guarded jealously. The most probable conclusion of experts in the field is that upon the prohibition of the activities of the Temple in 1307, this Great Secret, along with a good part of the enormous fortune accumulated by the Templars, was taken on board the phantom fleet of La Rochelle and carried to the dominion of the Sinclair clan in Scotland, where a generous refuge was offered to the fugitive knights. It is practically proved that a Sinclair (or Saint Clair), Grand Master of the clandestine Temple, joined the Italian sailors Nicolò and Antonio Zeno, completing a transatlantic voyage at the end of the fourteenth century that brought them to the coast of North America. They buried the treasure of the Great Secret in a pit on Oak Island, off the coast of Nova Scotia.

An old marine chronicle claims that when Captain Kidd captured the ship *Quedah Merchant* (which became his flagship) off India's Malabar coast in 1698, he received an ancient map from a mysterious passenger, showing the location of a small island with a Templar cross drawn on its interior. The possessor of this document assured Kidd that the cross marked the secret treasure trove of the Templars. From then on, all sufficiently knowledgeable corsairs began searching for "Captain Kidd's treasure," beginning with Kidd himself (the story found a literary variation in Robert Louis Stevenson's famous novel *Treasure Island*).

The Order of the Temple, which sometimes acted under the guise of Freemasonry, was the primary party interested in acquiring this map, in order to avoid letting the sacred relics fall into strange hands. Through mediators, the Order paid astronomical sums to hire the greatest pirate captains, some of whom had Freemason ancestors or belonged directly to this secret society.

The Templar Son of the Virgin Queen

Francis Drake's familiar surname is related to the word *dragon,* the mythical beast that was one of the Templars' emblems. It is also said that in his successful circumnavigation of the globe, Drake used the ancient maps of Egyptian and Chinese navigators that belonged to the Temple. Another story claims that the corsair's love affair with Queen Elizabeth resulted in a son who was raised by the Lord Keeper of the Great Seal, Sir Nicholas Bacon, who revealed the young man's origin to him upon his coming of age and gave him a sealed coffer containing the legacy of his true father. This son was none other than Francis Bacon, the great English philosopher who was accused of being an atheist and a Freemason. In his books, Bacon defended the importance of science over obscurantism—for example, in his treatise *Of the Proficience and Advancement of Learning* and in his *Novum Organum Scientiarum.* Shortly before his death, he wrote *The New Atlantis,* concerning a social and scientific utopia in which he described advances and inventions that would occur only centuries later, and an imaginary nation organized around higher moral and spiritual values. Were these prophecies part of the mysterious Templar legacy of Francis Drake? Was this perfect society, with the evocative name of New Atlantis, the Arcadia that the Templars hoped to establish in the New World? Bacon carried the answer to his grave. The work was published in 1627, a year after his death.

Other pirates and corsairs connected with Freemasonry are Henry Morgan, later the leader of the Masonic community of the Brotherhood of the Coast, subsidized by secretly Masonic personages such as the duke of Albemarle and Admiral Christopher Mings; and Captain Kidd, who may have received the map of the Oak Island treasure not entirely by accident. It is said that his patron, the duke of Bellomont, came from a French family of Templar origin, called Beaumont in France and Bellomonte in Italy and Spain. As for the pirate governor Woodes Rogers, some chronicles state that he was an agent of the Vatican, belonging to a fanatical Irish Catholic clan.

But the most difficult proof to refute concerning the close link between the Temple and piracy is the *Joyeux Roger,* or Jolly Roger, mentioned earlier, the flag hoisted by the Templar ships after their dispersion. The sign of the skull with an X formed by bones on a black background was not invented by the Templar mariners of La Rochelle, nor by the Sicilian king who hoisted it over his warships, nor by the relatives of the Scottish Templars upon whose gravestones it is carved. In fact, it was an ancient talismanic sign that the Temple adopted as the symbol of its fight against the Vatican. As is well known, the Jolly Roger was flown by the pirate ships of the corsair states, whose main aim was to attack the vessels of the Papal States in the Mediterranean and those of the devoutly Catholic kingdom of Spain in the Caribbean and Atlantic.

Of course, the rise of the golden age of piracy corresponded not only to the plans of the Templars, but also to more concrete interests, which promoted the emergence of the British Empire and the implementation of capitalism.

4

THE BRITISH EMPIRE AND THE PRIVATEERS

As we have seen in the preceding pages, the English political and economic elite of the seventeenth century openly encouraged and financed pirates, taking advantage of the benefits of their raids. The Crown negotiated with the corsairs, using them as irregular combatants in its wars against Spain and France. This complicity changed radically at the beginning of the eighteenth century, when this elite managed to push piracy to the margins of its imperial conquests, marking a strict distinction between corsair voyages and the expeditions of the Royal Navy and the merchant fleets that served the growing trade of the East and West India Companies.

The Vilification of the Corsairs

In 1707, England and Scotland united under a treaty forming the United Kingdom of Great Britain. This was the nascent British Empire, which began to colonize territories discovered or captured in North America, the West Indies, and the islands of the South Pacific. This imperialism required presenting the best possible image to other European kingdoms and the native governors and magnates of Britain's new possessions. Pirates did not fit this image, and the British powers used penal legislation, propaganda, and even popular literature to vilify piracy, while at the same time glorifying imperial occupation, colonial commerce, and the "civilizing" effects of imperialism.

However, the ethical and social differences between imperialism and piracy were much less apparent. The rigid, puritanical, and hierarchical English society of the era created a substantial and growing stratum of marginalized and unemployed people for whom the best way out was to go to sea and become pirates. Although it is true that the pirates' cruelty was atrocious to say the least, it was no worse than that of the imperialist sailors and merchants, who sold African slaves, exploited indigenous populations, and depleted natural resources. At the same time, many English corsairs and pirates drew maps and compiled geographical, nautical, and ethnographical information on the territories they reached, directly benefiting the explorers and scientists in the service of the Empire.

It should be remembered that in previous centuries the English navy and commercial fleets had concentrated their forces on protecting and furthering British interests in Europe and India, leaving conquest and colonization up to Spain. Only with the formation of the United Kingdom did the imperial project begin to take shape, starting with a cautious approach to the West Indies. Before this time, England's political and economic interests in the Caribbean had been almost exclusively in the hands of the pirates. They had sacked the coasts and islands of the region and put the transport of riches in check, sapping Spain's power and resources and filling the coffers of the Crown and other sly investors. Both the British government and the big merchants tacitly accepted the pirates' activity, granting them corsair patents and organizing expeditions of so-called privateers—captains with their own ships who acted as pirates in the service of others. The British excuse for attacking Spanish ships and possessions, even in times past, was that Philip II had tried to invade England in 1588 and, above all, that Spain had built a colonial empire without precedent, destroying the delicate balance of power among European forces.

The privateers transported goods as compensation for the Spanish merchant ships that sailed armed, with captains and crews trained for combat. They also served those who hired them to "clean up" the bad reputation Britain had acquired for aiding the bandits of the sea, for which purpose they maintained a strict distinction between privateers, who rendered a legal service to the Crown, and pirates, mere criminals

Portrait of Philip II by Antonio Moro, Royal Monastery of San Lorenzo de El Escorial, Madrid.

who acted outside the law. Possibly, however, the true motive was that the privateers had to hand over a large percentage of their booty by contract, whereas the pirates got to keep it all.

What is certain is that the English government patronized and made use of both privateers and pirates, and that in practice the privateers operated with the same brutality and impiety as the independent pirates. Such activity was equally common among the captains and officers of the British navy during its imperial expansion. It should be remembered that between the sixteenth and eighteenth centuries, a bloody and merciless war went on throughout the world's seas over the riches of America and Asia, and that all those who participated in it acted with terrible cruelty, whatever their character, title, rank, or job might be.

Sir Walter Raleigh and the Treasure of El Dorado

Sir Walter Raleigh was a particularly unusual privateer in that he financed his expeditions with his abundant personal fortune. He shared with Francis Drake the honor of being one of the favorite corsairs of Queen Elizabeth I, and although he was just as much a pirate as any other English corsair sailing the Caribbean, the Indian Ocean, or the South Pacific, British historians always prefer to remember him as an explorer, cartographer, and colonist in the service of the Empire.

Raleigh's link with the Templars is evident, since he resided at one of the Order's offices during a prolonged stay in France. He also offered his help to the young Huguenot king of Navarre Henry of Bourbon in his aspirations to the French throne, and was in Paris during the Saint Bartholomew's Day massacre in 1576, perhaps to protect the future Henry IV should he be threatened. Raleigh must have known at least part of the secret legend claiming that the treasure of the Temple was hidden in America. In 1595, he heard rumors about a secret place in the dense jungles of Guyana, known as El Dorado (The Golden) for the splendid abundance of this metal. Sir Walter had no doubt that the gold in question was the

Walter Raleigh, after failing in his New World colonies and the Virginia coast, set his sights on new goals. From Sarmiento de Gamboa he had heard the legend of a land rich in gold in the middle of the South American jungle, near the mouth of the Orinoco River: El Dorado.

Templar treasure, and organized a zealous expedition in search of it. They did not find it, perhaps because El Dorado did not exist and was only a hoax devised by the natives to rid themselves of the Englishmen.

His Majesty's Informers

Whereas Spain held almost all the important colonial settlements in the West Indies and the South Seas, the more or less scientific reports of the pirates and corsairs of the seventeenth century resulted in valuable information for the imperial interests of Great Britain during the following century. Some pirates obtained pardons by publishing personal diaries, binnacle logs, and records of voyages, which served as guides for the expansionist campaigns of the Royal Navy. This work of geographical espionage was continued by the privateers, who even took scientists along on their expeditions. The most noteworthy ex-pirate authors of the eighteenth century were William Dampier and John Esquemeling, whose works are still consulted by historians today. In the preface to his *Buccaneers of America,* Esquemeling proclaims that his book offers "exact descriptions and maps of South Seas ports, harbors, rivers, creeks, islands, rocks, towns, and cities" from the regions that he visited on his voyages. For his part, Dampier writes in *A New Voyage Round the World* that he abandoned piracy to write with "a hearty zeal for the promoting of useful knowledge, and of anything that may . . . tend to my country's advantage." The information given by Dampier proved so fundamental for Britain's imperial ambitions that the recently created Royal Society took the author under its wing and quickly elected him its president.

Having obtained definitive and secure control of its possessions in the East Indies, England was able to take aggressive action upon the American territories controlled by Spain. Surmounting the internal dissensions that had caused almost a century of political, social, and religious conflict, the British came together, for the first time in many years, in massive patriotic support of the imperial project. Many enlisted in the navy or embarked with the privateers, just as much to conquer and colonize new lands as to destroy the Spanish Empire and expand throughout the world the anti-Catholic, xenophobic, and authoritarian behavior characterizing the House of Hanover that now reigned over England. As a historian with a sense of humor wrote, "[F]or the Empire, the human species was divided into Britons and natives," the latter including all those who were different from and strange to the inhabitants of the British Isles and their pioneers overseas. The "natives" of these lands were considered inferior and available for dominating, exploiting, torturing, enslaving, and raping.

It soon became common for African slaves to escape from British colonial plantations in North America, the Caribbean, and the South Seas by joining pirate expeditions. As has been explained, the laws of piracy were much more democratic than European legislation, and made no distinctions of religion, race, occupation, or social rank in previous life. Black crewmen habitually sailed on pirate ships, and many were elected to command them.

Englishwomen were not "natives," but the prejudice and sexist conceit of the imperial era subjected them to possessive and degrading domination. Respected historians state that Anne Bonny and Mary Read are only two examples of the many women who chose piracy as a form of liberation, and some claim that Bartholomew Roberts himself was actually a woman in disguise. The pirates accepted any "man" who wanted to join them in the fight, neither asking who or what he was, nor subjecting him to medical examinations. Once on board it was common for the women to keep wearing men's clothing—not in order to continue hiding their sex, but because the women's clothing of the time was not appropriate for sailor's work or hand-to-hand combat. They were all proud to be pirates, and no record exists of any woman pirate who, when captured, pretended to be a hostage in order to escape punishment.

But at the beginning of the imperial conquests, warships and merchantmen replaced pirate ships, while the Royal Navy, the East and West India Companies, and the Royal Society reclaimed them from the British government that banned and persecuted them.

Under the Veil of the Royal Society

It is worth discussing briefly the role played by the Royal Society in this epoch. This prestigious and respected nongovernmental organization, dedicated to promoting and furthering scientific research, was completely at the service of the imperialist project, sending out explorers and experts whenever Great Britain needed information on the territories it had conquered or intended to conquer. Under the impartial cloak of science, hundreds of geographers, surveyors, cartographers, botanists, meteorologists, and other specialists sent abroad and financed by the Royal Society worked to provide valuable data for the colonial empire. This scientific organization also backed the profitable voyages of the adventuring navigator James Cook, who passed for a disinterested explorer. In the nineteenth century, the society sponsored missionaries (such as David Livingstone in Africa) who attempted to catechize the natives and, deliberately or otherwise, explored new territories that the British Empire then appropriated, exploiting their inhabitants.

The grand plan of the imperialists in gaining the support of the British population and the admiration of other European nations was the pompous and wearisome propaganda known as the three C's: Civilization, Christianity, and Commerce. But, in fact, Britain was only truly interested in the third item, the other two simply serving as a vehicle and a cover for the consolidation of its power in overseas colonies. Pirates, on the other hand, did not consider themselves civilized, were not at all Christian, and disrupted commerce, attacking merchant convoys and seizing their cargo. The Empire no longer needed to hire privateers, much less tolerate the illegal activity of pirates and buccaneers. Those formerly admired romantic heroes of the sea were expelled from the scene without a second thought and replaced by navy commanders and merchant captains who acted with equal or greater cruelty, serving their own ends. As Daniel Defoe wrote through his character Captain Bellamy: "They vilify us, the scoundrels do, when there is only this difference, they rob the poor under the cover of law, forsooth, and we plunder the rich under the protection of our own courage."

The crews of the few pirate ships that continued in action after 1720 in the Caribbean and the South Seas preserved their democratic structures of command, their equal division of the booty, and their ethic of solidarity as established by the Brotherhood of the Coast.

PART 3
THE ORDER OF THE TEMPLE AND FREEMASONRY

5

THE SECRET LODGE
OF THE
STONEWORKERS

Experts on the subject of secret societies tend to believe that the Order of the Temple, after its prohibition, established Freemasonry as a cover and an instrument for continuing its activities. Others, better informed, hold that at its peak in the twelfth century, when it sponsored the construction of Gothic cathedrals, the Order infiltrated the trade of the stoneworkers and instilled its secrecy in them in order to prevent the release of the secret ancient architectural techniques used in these works. Other schools of thought maintain that Freemasonry was an occultist brotherhood, much more ancient and full of tradition than the "poor knights of the Temple." The relationship between the two societies will always remain a subject of speculation and controversy.

The origins of Freemasonry are hazy, with theories reaching from the beginning of time to the foundation of the Grand Lodge of London in 1717. Perhaps the order's beginning was neither so long ago nor so recent, the truth lying instead in one of the theories that situate it in some intermediate epoch of human history. In any case, popular imagination and the Freemasons themselves have always linked Freemasonry to the stoneworkers, whose trade is known as *maçonnerie* in French. Some scholars explain that these stoneworkers were admired and respected in all eras for being the builders of the most symbolic and imposing structures: pyramids, pantheons, temples, sanctuaries, fortifications, basilicas, castles, and cathedrals. They held knowledge permitting them to erect these sturdy edifices, building high gates, dividing the interiors into rooms, and covering them with roofs to keep out the weather. To other artisans, these abilities were the object of envy, and to the common people, something magical. Perhaps the *maçons* themselves got to the point of considering themselves a bit magical, or at least allowing themselves to be surrounded with the aura of mystery and occultism that the popular imagination conferred upon them.

The Era of the Cathedrals

In the case of the medieval cathedral builders, a practical and rational explanation exists for their having formed brotherhoods more or less secret in character. The idea originated in the *loges,* or lodges, which were initially nothing esoteric, simply the huts or temporary structures that the stoneworkers put up around the buildings they were constructing. They used these enclosures for storing their tools and work clothes, for meeting to discuss trade matters, for working on smaller tasks in bad weather, and for lodging those workers who had nowhere else to stay. As time went on, conversations in the lodges began to revolve around the necessity of protecting professional knowledge from infiltration and preventing certain apprentices from passing themselves off as experts. The stoneworkers then began to create the *loges de la maçonnerie,* brotherly guilds whose purpose was to monitor the quality of the work and the expertise for which they were hired, as well as to ensure that their patrons provided them with good labor conditions and payment in accord with their abilities. Other artisans formed similar societies, but the stoneworkers were remarkable for the rigidity of their rules and their strict organization into successive levels of authority, as well as for their faithful secrecy regarding the techniques and procedures of the trade. This version of the story is the most accepted and widespread, but also faces some noteworthy objections. The most pressing one is that in French, *maçonner* also means to enclose or block off something; therefore, a group that wished to remain occult might have adopted this name as a metaphor. Another interesting objection presented is the question: Why did a brotherly guild of manual artisans need to introduce into its rules, and follow to the letter, a moral and ethical ideology that was absolutely rigorous, indeed appropriate for a monastic order? Perhaps the answer lies in its relationship with the Templars.

Historians generally accept that the Order of the Temple played a decisive role in the construction of Gothic cathedrals in France in the twelfth century. In many of these constructions they made use of unusual resources and techniques, such as ogival arches and octagonal shapes. Obviously, starting with no prior knowledge, it was necessary for the Templars to make deals and contracts with stoneworkers guilds in order to build such enormous and magnificent architectural works. The construction of a cathedral would take decades and even sometimes centuries, during which time the Templars and masons had to deal with each other on an almost daily basis. It was not uncommon for them to exchange some aspects of their respective brotherhoods, and to

Chapel of the Templars in Laon (Aisne).

make various forms of mutual commitments. The Temple had no choice but to share the secret techniques of construction that it wanted to use with the Grand Masters, requiring in exchange that the principles of the stoneworkers' lodges include loyalty, solidarity, and respect for the promise of secrecy. The masons, for their part, required the Templars to agree to hire only stoneworkers of whom they approved, and only according to the conditions and fees that they had established. It is probable that the relationship went no further at this time, and that the two parties maintained an amicable professional relationship until the last few years of the thirteenth century; but as has been described, the Templars had to flee in desperation from the persecutions of the Inquisition and the troops of Philip the Fair in 1307. It is logical enough that those who could not escape France sought refuge among their stoneworker friends, knowing that they would be protected by the secret nature of masonry.

For many scholars, the close bond between Templars and masons begins at this time, and for some this link leads to the total absorption of the brotherhood of stoneworkers into the Order of the Temple. For the latter, it was essential to maintain the secret organization, authority, and discipline necessary for continuing their mission in such difficult times. The structure of Freemasonry fit these requirements perfectly.

Stoneworkers, sculptors, water carriers . . . detail from a miniature by Jean Fouquet.

Masonic symbols from the Scottish Rite (clockwise from left). The first is of the sixth degree: Intimate Secretary; the second is of the eleventh degree: Sublime Knight Elected; the third is of the twenty-second degree: Knight of the Royal Axe; and the fourth is of the twenty-third: Chief of the Tabernacle.

Up to this point, we have summarized the canonical explanation of the birth of Freemasonry and its link to the Templars, which agrees fairly well with historical accounts and surviving documents and testimonies. But there are other versions of the story that go much deeper in their esotericism; we shall describe them as we continue.

The Mythical Origins of Freemasonry

The prehistoric megalithic cultures were the first to build monuments of stone, and therefore they were also the origin of the first stoneworkers. One theory that has not been disproved claims that these primitive communities had elaborate knowledge of various sciences, perhaps inherited from mythical antediluvian civilizations such as those of Atlantis and Arcadia. It has been suggested recently that the astrologers and megalithic stoneworkers established a special Hermetic caste in order not to lose the magic powers bestowed upon them through their knowledge. Their ability to measure celestial movements and determine the course of the seasons was astounding to their contemporaries, since it allowed them to predict the times for sowing, harvest, and the rains—fundamental information for planning the simple activities of every day and even for the community's survival. This caste of priestly scientists built various astronomical observatories out of stone, such as those of Newgrange and Stonehenge. Obviously, to avoid imitation by others, they had to incorporate the stoneworkers into their elite, or at least make alliances with them.

The *Book of Enoch,* found among the Dead Sea Scrolls at Qumran, explains the scientific principles used by the stone observatories, which it calls "Uriel's machines." It is known that those Masonic lodges that are considered authentic attribute their origin and inspiration to the Dead Sea Scrolls. The megalithic priests predicted the collision of a comet with Earth in 3150 BC, and they emigrated to the east, taking their secret knowledge with them. The *Book of Enoch* tells how the comet indeed collided with our planet, causing the great inundation that we know as the Deluge.

According to what was deciphered from one of the copper Dead Sea Scrolls, many members of the brotherhood of stoneworkers survived the

French painting from 1740 in which a recent initiate to Freemasonry is welcomed.

catastrophe and preserved their occult knowledge, imparting it to some of the wise Hebrew descendants of Noah. From this basis the mysterious Zadokite cult was formed, combining antediluvian wisdom with the lineage of King David. When the Romans expelled the Zadokite priests from Jerusalem in AD 70, the priests managed to bury their documents and relics beneath the ruins of the Temple of Solomon. The descendants of these precursors of Freemasonry—the knights who founded the Order of the Temple in 1099—unearthed the Great Secret. In order for the Templars to reestablish the age-old Masonic brotherhood, all that was required was for the Order to be prohibited and persecuted at the beginning of the fourteenth century.

Freemasonry preserves a rich imagery of symbols and engravings relating to the construction of the Temple of Solomon in 945 BC by builders and stoneworkers from the city of Tyre. Some authors use this fact to trace the origins of the Masonic brotherhood back to the Phoenician sects that guarded the secrets of stone construction. Indeed, the artisanship of stone was already well known in those days and in later epochs and civilizations, such as Greece, Rome, and Byzantium. The ancient Egyptians represented the virtues of truth and justice with the carpenter's square, an instrument that, together with the compass, forms the universal symbol of Masonic lodges. Confucius, around 500 BC, spoke of the goodness of acting "squarely," a term also used by Aristotle to designate honest actions. To consider these thinkers Freemasons would be absurd, but it is known that the square and the compass were the main instruments used by medieval stoneworkers—that is, the *maçons*.

The British Connection

Once he had subjugated the other, smaller British kingdoms, the legendary King Aethelstan of England brought together the most skilled stoneworkers to establish the Masonic Rite of York, consecrated by a royal charter in AD 926. The document permitted the stoneworkers to meet once a year, and it appears that among their functions was that of authorizing and overseeing the construction of numerous abbeys, castles, and fortifications. The importance given by Aethelstan to the masons is entirely confirmed in various documents of the epoch, such

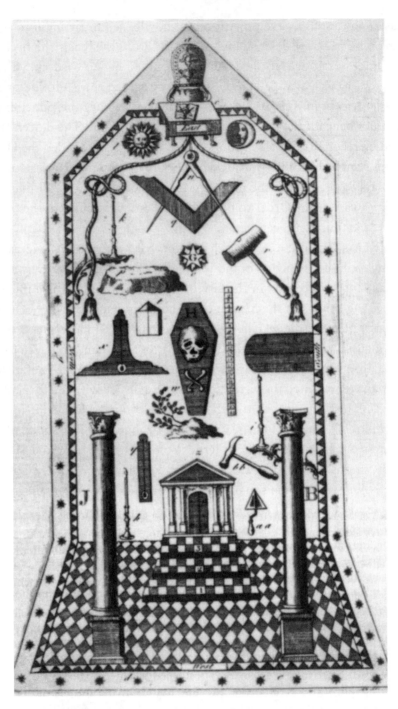

*French symbols uniting elements of Freemasonry and the Temple with
the variety of tools depicted (engraving from 1740).*

as the *Regius* and *Cooke* manuscripts. There is also incontestable evidence that active Masonic lodges operated in Scotland after 1057, and that those of England, continuing the tradition of Aethelstan, became official around 1220. Soon these lodges, societies, or *compagnonnages* (as they were called in France and by extension in continental Europe)

Self-portrait of Nicolas Poussin, 1650. In this painting Poussin wears a Mason's ring on the little finger of his right hand, and many right angles can be seen in the frames of the pictures in the background. (Louvre Museum.)

became abundant. Their outward function was to provide responsible and effective stoneworkers to fulfill the aspirations of the sovereigns and ecclesiastic leaders in their ambitious plans for construction. In this era, except for the king and the Church, travel and communication were highly restricted in England. The masons had to devise their own methods of recognizing each other to avoid intrusion or deception when moving from one workplace to the next. They obtained safe conduct for those members who had to attend two or more constructions at a time. All this is the material of speculation—some historians deny that there are any proofs of organized masonry in England, unlike in Scotland. Curiously, the name Scottish Rite was created in France many

Illustration of a French Masonic temple from the beginning of the nineteenth century.

centuries later, in 1737, by a group of exiled Scottish Freemasons, led by Andrew Ramsay.

Investigations of the birth and history of Freemasonry in Scotland inevitably revolve around the exploits of the Templars. After their disappearance upon the banning and persecution of their Order, some knights are believed to have sailed to the northern part of Great Britain, which Robert the Bruce had just made independent, for which reason Scotland had been excommunicated. As we shall see in more detail later, the Templars took refuge there to continue with their project, relatively safe from the Vatican and the Inquisition. There is no doubt that they took their treasures, relics, secrets, and ceremonies with them, as is confirmed by the testimonies found in Rosslyn Chapel.

The Remarkable Rosslyn Chapel

It is impossible to investigate the history of Freemasonry without making reference to the enigmatic Rosslyn Chapel, located a few miles south of Edinburgh. Its construction was begun in 1446 by the Scottish noble Sir William Sinclair, chief of a clan with a long Templar tradition going back to the first Grand Master, Hughes de Payns. The construction of the chapel took forty years, and it is profusely decorated with reliefs and inscriptions from Templar and Enochian imagery, including various Masonic symbols. It is said that in the fifteenth century, when books and documents might have been censored or burned, Sir William opted to have a coded message engraved in stone for future generations of initiates.

Among the more surprising elements visible is the Apprentice Pillar, an inscription describing various processes of initiation, and an ornate arch with a string of ears of corn, made half a century before Columbus's "discovery" of America.

In 1583, King James VI of Scotland (later James I of England) appointed William Schaw as the Master of the Work and Director General of Freemasonry. Five years later, Schaw issued his famous statute establishing the Freemasons' duties to their lodge. The statute also set penalties for unsatisfactory work and prohibited working with unqualified masons. In his second statute, in 1599, Schaw made the first veiled

The Apprentice Pillar, Rosslyn Chapel.

references to the presence of secret knowledge in the works of Freemasonry. These regulations also obliged the lodges to keep a written register and to meet at least once a year, introducing the Art of Memory into the tests for the initiates.

The Illustrious Invisible College

In the mid-seventeenth century, an eminent antiquarian named Elias Ashmole, knowledgeable in alchemy and the occult sciences, made connections with some of the important intellectuals of the period in order to interest them in Freemasonry. His meetings in the Compton Room at Canonbury Tower in London were attended by persons such as Robert Boyle, the father of scientific chemistry; Christopher Wren, the great architect and city planner; and Sir Isaac Newton, the genius physicist, mathematician, and astronomer. Soon afterward they decided to organize themselves into a secret society, which took the name "the Invisible College," with the objective of investigating esoteric knowledge and promoting exoterica—that is, scientific knowledge. In 1662, under the presidency of the Masonic Grand Master Francis Bacon, a well-known philosopher and diplomat, King Charles II granted his Royal Charter to the college, which suggests that it was not all that invisible.

Why did these thinkers, scientists, and artists become clandestine members of a mysterious organization like Freemasonry? At this time, science and philosophy were both involved in a covert struggle against irrationalism and religious dogma. Associating with Freemasonry meant obtaining the protection of the Church's greatest historical enemy, as well as being able to take advantage of its secrecy in order to act in as much safety as possible. It must be remembered that the Freemasons were not merely artisans who worked with stone, but also kings, nobles, and great magnates, all drawn in for the same reasons. The great minds of the era felt comfortable in such company, and acquired valuable complicity in their defense of rationalism.

Once Freemasonry acquired official status in 1717, its popularity extended rapidly throughout the United Kingdom, especially among the middle class, merchants, and military, as well as throughout the British colonies in America. In 1731, the Grand Lodge of Pennsylvania was formed, and it founded and promoted the numerous lodges that emerged in the following years throughout the colonies. As will be seen in a later chapter, Freemasonry played a decisive role in the independence of the United States, and the majority of the Founding Fathers were Freemasons, including Benjamin Franklin and George Washington. Throughout the eighteenth century, Freemasonry attracted notable personages in science, the arts, and politics, such as Mozart, Frederick the Great, and Robert Walpole.

Butting Heads with the Church

A significant factor in the history of the Freemasons is their constant dislike for the Catholic Church, perhaps further confirmation of their Templar origin. The Vatican expressly prohibited Freemasonry for the first time in Pope Clement XII's bull of 1738, and issued new condemnations in 1884. The Freemason was the phantom fought by preachers and clerics as the diabolical agent of evil, until Paul VI abolished all anti-Masonic bulls in 1974, perhaps as a result of attention to mutual interests that have since made the activity of the Holy See more tolerant.

However, the Church established anti-Masonic sentiment very firmly in the minds of its more devoted and ignorant faithful, by methods such as denouncing the Freemasons with papal bulls. The persistence of this sentiment was used by many populist and dictatorial politicians, among them Mussolini, Franco, and Hitler, to awaken the fanaticism of the masses in their favor.

Today, Masonic lodges are legal and registered entities, acting without subterfuge although not too openly, and their practice is not considered criminal in any Western country. The Rights of Man protect them in the majority of national constitutions, in the constitution of the European Union, and in the charter of the United Nations.

PART 4
THE TEMPLARS IN AMERICA

6

VOYAGES
OF ANTIQUITY

Today, hardly any serious historians still cling to the myth that Christopher Columbus discovered America, much less that he did so by accident. Apart from the fact that the famous navigator knew exactly where he was going, it is absurd to think that the many civilizations that sailed the seas over the millennia had never reached the coasts of the Americas. The first boats providing secure transport were built in the eighth millennium BC; and considerable development came thereafter, especially among the Egyptians, Phoenicians, Cretans, and Romans. These civilizations sailed all around the Mediterranean, the Red Sea, the African coastline, and the Indian Ocean, trading and building ports and colonial enclaves. It has been proved that Polynesian seafarers crossed the Pacific at least as far as Easter Island, and it is possible that Chinese and Arab navigators also sailed those waters.

As we know, the first centers of human population expanded from Africa throughout the world over hundreds of thousands of years. According to the traditionally accepted explanation, this expansion reached the isolated American continent by means of an initial group of some eighty individuals who crossed the Bering Strait, where at the time there was still a strip of land joining the two continents (the water that now separates them frozen in glaciers). For the last seventy-five years, official anthropology has claimed that these pioneers gave rise to all Native American ethnic groups, who developed without contact with the rest of the world until the providential arrival of Christopher Columbus.

The idea of the "discovery of America" at the end of the fifteenth century was implanted into written history in the West in the following centuries, and is consistent with the Eurocentrism of the imperial powers and their colonial prejudices. They could not accept the idea that the "New World," whose riches allowed them to build their empires, had not first been discovered, colonized, and civilized by the powerful and omniscient Europe, but had instead been explored centuries earlier by "marginal" and "ignorant" civilizations. Only a few decades ago, official history finally recognized that, as overwhelming proof demonstrates, the Viking Erik the Red reached Greenland and Newfoundland around the end of the tenth century. Even then, the Normans were not considered Europeans, and their accomplishment was reduced intentionally to having reached Greenland and maybe part of the American continent because they were "blown off course by a storm." But in the last few decades, new discoveries have been published, and investigations have been made demonstrating that the societies of antiquity were greater navigators, and traveled farther, than was believed before.

The Megalithic Navigators

The most surprising theory, tenaciously defended by its proponents, claims that the first people to arrive in Greenland were mariners from the megalithic culture—that is, the prehistoric people of Western Europe between the fourth and second millennia BC who, as mentioned earlier, built various monuments of stone, such as menhirs, monoliths, and dolmens, the function and significance of which are now the topic of debate. These primitive societies worshipped the sun, and it is believed that their priests thought the earth was a disk, like the sun and moon.

Recently deciphered stone inscriptions tell us that the entire known world was surrounded by a vast sea, and that to the west there was the "Empire of Death" at the edge of the world. The megalithic people seem to have been good navigators and excellent astronomers, paying homage to the sun by setting sail precisely from the Tropic of Cancer.

Various geographical designs found in their petroglyphs allow us to infer that they reached Atlantic archipelagos and islands such as the Canaries, Madeira, the Azores, Cape Verde, and the Faeroes.

Without doubt, the ships and the nautical expertise at their disposal did not make it an easy task for them to leave the coasts and navigate in the open seas, but it is possible that they also reached the islands of Saint Helena and Ascension in the South Atlantic, and that around 3200 BC, they reached Iceland and Greenland, either sailing bravely and blindly, or blown there by a tempest. The famous monument of Stonehenge was a sanctuary praising the sun for these discoveries, as well as a celestial observatory for making the calculations that allowed them to navigate by the stars.

Megalithic culture also developed in some regions of central Africa, with characteristics similar to those of Europe. Discoveries have been made there of great voyages reaching Madagascar and crossing the Indian Ocean all the way to Australia. Although it is hard to believe, some hold that these explorers later sailed from Polynesia to Hawaii and reached the Alaskan coast via the Bering Sea. Some more daring scholars claim that prehistoric Africans crossed the Atlantic with the aid of primitive compasses around 2200 BC. Pushed forward by winds and favorable currents, they sailed to South America, continued north to Bermuda, and then explored North America. The main argument supporting this theory

Ancient cultures believed that the Atlantic was populated by terrible sea monsters.

is the discovery of the remains of a small megalithic colony in New England, and other evidence scattered along the banks of the Ohio River.

Another recent proposal places the first transatlantic voyages in the ice age that chilled the planet during the Late Paleolithic, 13,000 years ago. Its proponents claim that the tribes of the extreme north of Canada were able to make contact with the European civilizations of the so-called Aurignacian culture thanks to a swift drop in the earth's temperature. This phenomenon, destroying vegetation and causing the extinction or migration of animal species, dramatically reduced the means of subsistence. People therefore made occasional voyages to the southeast to fish and get fresh water. They may have gone in canoes such as those used by present-day Inuit people, negotiating passages through the frozen sea, or even floating on chunks of ice driven along by marine currents. In any case, the defenders of these voyages do not claim that these American visitors reached Europe, making it difficult to prove the correctness of their theory.

Solomon and the Phoenician Mariners

The reader will remember that the Templars founded their Order at the place where the Temple of Solomon had once stood. Excavations at this site have found objects and documents going back to biblical times. Why not also ancient sea maps drawn by Hebrew cartographers? "King Solomon's Mines" were an established tradition in the Levant, their fabulous riches tempting plenty of European explorers. The Bible does not mention them, but the Book of Kings tells how Solomon went to his neighbor and ally, King Hiram of Tyre, offering him a fleet with which his navigators could sail the Levant in search of a legendary region known as Ophir, famous for its riches. The Phoenicians, excellent mariners, departed from the port of Ezion Geber on the Red Sea. For three years nothing was heard of this fleet, until it reappeared in the Mediterranean, arriving at the port of Tyre weighed down with gold, silver, ivory, precious gems, spices, and incense. The Bible does not explain how the Phoenicians obtained these valuable treasures, but we can guess that they were not above piracy at the time.

Some scholars have stated that the Greek translators connected the biblical Ophir with Sofir, the ancient Coptic name for India, renowned for its immense riches. The argument is worth considering, but why did the Phoenician sailors take three years to go to India and back? And above all, how did they leave from the Red Sea and arrive by the Mediterranean? In these times the Suez Canal did not exist, and the only possible way was to go around Africa (or in the opposite direction, all the way around the world). Historically, there is no record of the Phoenicians or any other people of the time being able to make such voyages. The great scene of Phoenician navigation was the Mediterranean, a sea that they sailed practically at whim, marking out trade routes and founding colonies on coasts and islands, among them Carthage, established at the end of the ninth century BC in North Africa (present-day Tunisia).

At the beginning of the second century AD, Plutarch, in one of his lesser-known writings, cited a document found in the ruins of Carthage. The anonymous author of this document said that the Carthaginians knew of an "actual continent" located a great distance to the west of the British Isles, and that the Phoenicians who reached its coasts had interbred with the native populations. It added that these racially mixed people made fun of Europeans because they lived "on a little island" compared to their vast continent, which spanned the entire western Atlantic. A century earlier, the Greek historian Diodorus had written that the Carthaginians "owned a great island, very far off in the ocean," where there were many mountains, navigable rivers, and natural riches. The

---

THE CARTHAGINIANS IN THE CANARY ISLANDS

Historians have not been able to establish the location of the Phoenician colony of Cerne, founded by the Carthaginian Hanno in the sixth century BC. Some locate it in the Canary Islands, based on documents telling of the arrival of the Portuguese in the fourteenth century. The Guanches, natives of the islands, were descended from a mix of an ancient African migration and a later influx of people who, according to reliable chronicles, came from the Mediterranean. The Portuguese sailors were surprised to find that the Guanches had fair skin and kept written documents that, oddly, they could not read themselves. The natives asked the conquerors if they could decipher them, but in keeping with the customs of the time, the Portuguese massacred the natives and burned their documents, believing them to be heretical texts.

same author explained how they had discovered this land "by accident" when a great storm blew them out to sea while they were sailing along the African coast establishing new colonies, and that they kept their discovery secret. In 1488, a French mariner named Jean Cousin had the same "accident" and ended up on the coast of Brazil. This occurred shortly before Columbus's voyage, and was registered in the annals of navigation of the port of Dieppe, in France.

Returning to Solomon's fleet: The Bible says that the ships reached Ophir and returned laden with gold. It is possible that in truth the Phoenician admiral, disappointed at not finding this mythical region, decided to return to Tyre, attempting to go around Africa via the Cape of Good Hope, but once his ships reached the Atlantic, the Benguela ocean current carried them out to the South American equatorial zone. Returning to the Mediterranean bearing the remarkable news would have been easy enough, riding the powerful Gulf Stream that runs from west to east. This would explain the "great island" described by Diodorus, which Solomon's cartographers drew but concealed at the order of King Hiram, hiding the map in the catacombs of the Temple where the Templars finally found it. All this would have occurred over the course of two millennia, allowing time for the legend of "King Solomon's Mines" to grow. The English author H. Rider Haggard published a novel with this title in 1886, placing these fabulous riches not in America, but in the heart of Africa—perhaps to stimulate the ambition of explorers in the service of the British Empire.

A Well-Known New World

Since official history has lowered its guard and no longer defends the theory of American isolation, many academic works on various "discoveries" of America before the arrival of Christopher Columbus have begun to surface. The list, of variable credibility, includes voyages undertaken by Egyptians, Sumerians, Phoenicians, Romans, Arabs, Chinese, and of course the Venetian Zeno brothers, the Scottish Templars themselves, and a few more questionable medieval navigators. Notable among them is the Irish monk Saint Brendan the Navigator, who, according to a legend of the High Middle Ages, crossed the ocean in a boat made of hide and found a "promised land" full of marvels. (In 1977, an expedition sponsored by *National Geographic* repeated this voyage in a similar boat, proving that it was nautically possible.) The Welsh Prince Madawg ab Owain Gwynedd, known as Madoc, sailed to the west in 1170 and discovered a beautiful and fertile land. Before returning, he left 120 of his men there, and in 1174 he made a second expedition with more ships and many colonists, including women and children. Nothing further is known of Madoc and his companions. The history could seem improbable, but recent DNA testing and comparative linguistic studies appear to demonstrate that the Mandan Sioux tribe in South Dakota is descended from those vanished Welsh colonists.

There are also reports of a possible transatlantic migration by the Albans, a Celtic tribe for which England was sometimes known as Albion. It is believed that these peaceful denizens of the British Isles lived in terror of Viking attacks, and that in order to escape them, they set sail for the west. They reached Iceland and later Greenland, finally arriving in Newfoundland and the Ungava Peninsula (or New Québec) in Canada. There, they interbred with the native population, losing their origin and their language.

The Route of the Codfish

In the historical archives of Lisbon, it is written that in 1472 the Portuguese navigator João Vaz Corte-Real was honored with the title of "Discoverer of the Land of the Codfish." It is highly probable that this royal distinction referred to the coast of Newfoundland, where these fish abound. The presence of Basque, Welsh, Portuguese, and Breton whalers and fishermen in these waters before Columbus's voyage has been confirmed. Apparently the natives called this type of teleost fish *baccaloa,* and they were so abundant as to almost hinder the movement of the European fishing vessels. The same word appears in various spellings in various documents. It is believed to be of Basque origin and was adopted early on by the Spanish and Portuguese, turning with time into the word *bacalao.* The fact that Native Americans also used the word suggests that long and frequent fishing trips were made across the Atlantic, following the route of the cod.

7

THE TEMPLARS' TRANSATLANTIC VOYAGE

Nicolò Zeno was a noble and rich Venetian navigator, connected with the Order of the Temple, who took a voyage to England around 1380 on a diplomatic mission. Venice had replaced Genoa as the major power in the Mediterranean, and the Venetians planned to extend their mercantile domination to other waters. The Templars, highly influential in Venice, wanted to make contact with their northern branch in Scotland, in whose custody the Great Secret was held. Thus, openly or secretly, they aided Zeno's expedition, whose official purpose was to open new trade routes along the European Atlantic coast. The Venetian navigator skirted Great Britain and arrived at the Faeroe Islands, where he was received by Henry Sinclair, prince of the Orkneys, descendant of the prestigious Templar lineage of the Saint Clair and Grand Master of the Order, whose knights had arrived on these islands almost a century before in one of the squadrons of the fleet of La Rochelle.

Henry Sinclair was born in 1345 in the famous Rosslyn castle in the north of Scotland, and was now a mature man. His lineage went back to the ninth century, when King Haakon VI, of Norway, granted a Sinclair the earldom of Orkney and the lordship of Shetland, which then included the Faeroe Islands. One of Sinclair's ancestors had fought in the crusades along with Godfrey de Bouillon, and was probably one of the founding knights of the Temple. Upon the dissolution of the Order, another Sinclair guided some of the Templar ships to Scotland, where they founded the first Masonic lodge.

Upon Zeno's arrival, the great preoccupation of Henry Sinclair, as Grand Master of Scottish freemasonry, was to find a permanent hiding place for the Great Secret, which was provisionally stashed in the vaults of Rosslyn. He wanted to transfer it to some place so remote and so unknown that it would be completely safe from the persecution of the Vatican and its military wing, the Hospitallers or Knights of Malta. Considering that the people of the Faeroes were of Norman origin, Sinclair was well informed of the voyages made by Erik the Red and his sons to Greenland and the other land farther to the west, which they had named Vinland due to the abundance of wild vines there. Sinclair received the Venetian voyager most cordially, and gave him lodging in his castle. In one late-night conversation, Nicolò explained the true character of his mission, and Henry Sinclair told him of his delayed plan to repeat the Viking voyages to the west.

Nicolò Zeno then wrote to his brother Antonio, a mariner with at least as much experience as Nicolò. Antonio arrived a few months afterward, taking advantage of Henry Sinclair's generous hospitality. Together, the three of them planned the transatlantic expedition meticulously, using

The Templar Castle of Rosslyn.

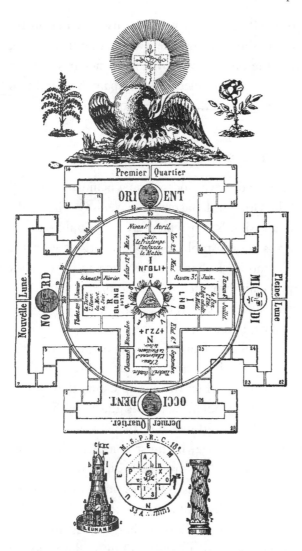

Mystic diagram of the Temple of Solomon, drawn by Templar knights following the scheme of the prophecy of Ezekiel.

the accounts of Norman mariners and some mysterious maps that were in the Grand Master's possession. On April 1, 1398, Sinclair, his lieutenant James Gunn, and the Zeno brothers set sail westward into the Atlantic with thirteen ships and three-hundred Templar knights. The voyage must not have taken very long, since this time there were no storms to blow them off course. They arrived on the coast of the land that the Vikings knew as Vinland—that is, present-day Nova Scotia, in Canada. Sinclair was enthralled by this region, and decided to settle there. Nicolò and some of the knights expressed their desire to return, and the Grand

Master, following a law of the Temple that was later used by the Brothers of the Coast, did not retain them against their will but let them leave, handing over the ships and the necessary provisions. Sinclair stayed in Vinland with the Templars who had decided to accompany him and two ships, one commanded by himself and the other by Antonio Zeno.

The Secret of Oak Island

The settlement that Sinclair founded was located on a peninsula flanked by two rivers, now called the Gold and Gaspereau Rivers. On the banks of each river were two small islands, on which grew the only oaks in all of Vinland. The explorers soon established good relations with the natives of the area, the Algonquin Indians of the Micmac tribe. They called Sinclair "Glooscap," which in their language meant something like "White God." It seems likely that other "white gods," probably Erik the Red or one of his sons, had arrived by sea earlier.

The Micmac told the Templars of marvelous lands farther to the south, which stimulated Henry Sinclair's adventurous spirit. At the end of the winter, he told Antonio that when the spring came, they would leave in search of these lands; but Sinclair, who was guarding the Great Secret in a kind of small fort built within the settlement, decided that before leaving on another risky voyage, he must complete the sacred mission for which he had come there. He ordered his men to dig a deep well next to the oak on one of the islands (Oak Island), at the bottom of which they would deposit a sealed container with the documents, mysteries, relics, and coffers full of gold coins that formed the Templar treasure (estimated at no less than £2,000,000 in modern money, and perhaps much more). They installed ingenious traps and devices in the shaft of the well, apparently making use of subterranean lakes and slabs of solid rock, so that no one who dug in the place would suspect that there was anything underneath. This complicated hiding place later gave rise to the famous legend of the "Well of Money" or "Treasure Island," mixed up with similar stories of pirates' booty (which, in fact, formed part of the Templars' treasure). Perhaps it is no coincidence that this part of Canada acquired the name of Sinclair's homeland, or that its modern-day capital is named Halifax, which was the earl's title of

Charles Montague, Lord Treasurer and first British prime minister, who founded the Bank of England in 1694.

The expedition then headed south, landing somewhat north of present-day Boston in what is now New England. They decided to settle there for a while and explore the surroundings, despite a rather unfriendly reception from the natives. At one point the Indians attacked the encampment and killed several of the explorers, among them Lieutenant James Gunn, who was Sinclair's cousin. The noble Templar was buried with all honors at Prospect Hull, near what is now Westford, Massachusetts. Even today, one can still see a gravestone there with a Templar-style carving depicting a medieval knight bearing the arms of the Gunn clan on his escutcheon. Henry Sinclair later returned to Scotland to fight the English invaders, and died in combat in 1401.

"Zeno's Narrative"

Nicolò Zeno died in 1395, leaving a series of notes and cartographical drawings of the voyages that he and his brother had undertaken with Henry Sinclair. Antonio compiled these writings, adding material that he had gathered himself and other information obtained from the Norman fishermen and mariners, handed down from generation to generation. He then sent all these documents and maps to his other brother, Carlo, who was then admiral of Venice. Carlo kept the volume in the archive of family history without appreciating its importance, perhaps without even reading it. The story of those fantastic travels in American lands was forgotten for more than a century and a half, damaged by humidity and rodents.

In 1558, a member of the Zeno family, also called Carlo, accidentally discovered this archive. The pages crumbled in his hands as he leafed through his ancestor's narration. Later, Carlo begged forgiveness for his stupidity, but at the time was astounded by the great importance of what remained of the document. He resolved to make it known in an impressive form, and published it under the title *Narrazione Zeno*. The book caused a sensation at the time, was translated into several European languages, and sparked bitter controversies regarding its authenticity. Carlo Zeno was accused of having published an apocryphal document based on the information of Columbus and Vespucci, but at this time no European navigator had gotten as far north as the coasts of New England and Nova Scotia, which were not explored again until the Englishman John Smith went there in 1612.

Antonio Zeno's remarkable writings explain the motivation for his and Henry Sinclair's intrepid voyage. An ancient Norman tale told of a boat full of fishermen from Frisland (Iceland?) that got caught in one of those storms that abound in fishermen's stories, and was blown far out to the west. They arrived at a land called Estotiland, whose inhabitants traded with the merchants of Engronenland (Greenland). Estotiland was a very fertile land with high mountains in the interior. The chief of the natives owned some secret books written in Latin, which he had obtained from his ancestors but could not read. The Estotilanders convinced their visitors to journey with them to the south, where they reached some extraordinary lands. The Europeans embarked on this route and arrived on the coast of a place called Drogeo or Droceo. There, a warlike aboriginal tribe attacked them, killing all the explorers except one. For some reason, the attackers spared the life of this young fisherman, keeping him as a slave for some years. Finally, he managed to escape, and after many adventures he reached Greenland and, from there, the Faeroe Islands. It is highly probable that this story, told in the *Narrazione Zeno*, combines various voyages of different navigators into

THE SAVAGE AND THE CIVILIZED

The story of the captured sailor describes the land called Drogeo as an enormous country, almost a new world, located very far to the south. It adds that this land was inhabited by many savage tribes who lived by hunting and dressed themselves in hides, continually fighting with each other. But it tells of encountering more civilized nations farther south where people worked with metals and built temples similar to European castles—although they had the disagreeable custom of killing prisoners in order to sacrifice their hearts to their gods. This description, dating back at least to the fourteenth century, is very similar to that of the chroniclers who accompanied the Spanish conquistadors to the Aztec and Mayan lands.

a single story in order to facilitate the oral transmission of its essential content: the existence of great fertile and inhabited lands on the other side of the ocean.

The *Narrazione Zeno* does not mention the Order of the Temple or Masonry, out of obvious respect for the clandestine nature of both. Less easily explained is the fact that it presents Henry Sinclair under the name Zichmni, considering that Sinclair was a sovereign publicly known in all of Europe. Perhaps the final editor, Carlo Zeno, had political reasons for not naming him, or maybe Carlo's ancestors used a name given to Sinclair by his subjects in the old Norman language, also motivated by excessive secrecy. In any case, later investigations have established with no room for doubt that "Zichmni" was the prince of the Orkneys, Henry Sinclair.

The document includes only a partial description of the voyages of Sinclair and the Venetian brothers, although it tells of the most important moments:

> So we brought our barks and our boats in to land, and we entered an excellent harbor, and we saw in the distance a great mountain that poured out smoke. . . . There were great multitudes of people, half-wild and living in caves. These were very small of stature and very timid; for when they saw our people, they fled into their holes. . . . When Zichmni heard this and noticed that the place had a wholesome and pure atmosphere, a fertile soil and good rivers and so many other attractions, he conceived the idea of staying there and founding a city.

Would this city have been the "New Jerusalem," the final objective of the millenary mission of the Templars? Of course, the *Narrazione Zeno* does not clarify this, and Sinclair only built a castle there, whose ruins are now a mecca for scholars and investigators of the enigmatic history of the Order of the Temple.

Among the Zeno brothers' documents are guidelines for a map of Greenland, which Carlo Zeno had a cartographer draw for inclusion in the book. It is said that this map is actually a copy of an older one, drawn by the Viking navigators or even by the mysterious cartographers

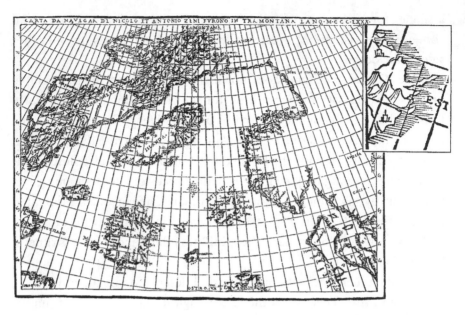

The navigational map of Nicolò and Antonio Zeno with a magnification showing two castles, representing conquests. Note that the two castles are one degree apart in latitude.

of many millennia ago, whose maps were in the possession of the Temple. Whatever the true origin of its drawing, what is certain is that it came to light for the first time with the *Narrazione Zeno,* that recent studies confirm the authorship of the Venetian navigators, and that this map was the principal guide used for navigating the coasts of the North Atlantic for the next 150 years.

A Well-Hidden Treasure

As has been related, the scholars who have studied the history of the Order of the Temple maintain that Henry Sinclair, Grand Master of the Scottish lodge, hid the Great Secret of the Templars in a deep well on an island off the coast of Nova Scotia. The reader may or may not believe this story, but what is certain is that an island with a solitary oak, appropriately named Oak Island, exists in Nova Scotia. Next to the old tree is a deep and ancient well, completely blocked off. Since the nineteenth century, it has been visited by legions of treasure hunters, including the

Canadian government, private companies formed specifically for this purpose, and individuals drawn from all over the world.

Since three teenagers accidentally discovered the well on Oak Island more than two centuries ago, its legend has given rise to many stories of ambition and frustration. Among the more distinguished treasure hunters were Franklin D. Roosevelt, future president of the United States, who founded a company called Old Gold Salvage in 1909 with the exclusive purpose of excavating the well; and the actor Errol Flynn, famous pirate of the silver screen, who set out on a similar mission in 1940, but had to stop because the rights to seek the treasure had been purchased by his colleague John Wayne.

The origin of the alleged fabulous treasure lying at the bottom of the well took various forms in the popular imagination. Apart from the origin detailed in this book, attributing it to the Order of the Temple, one explanation claims that this was Captain Kidd's treasure. We should remember that William Kidd received a map from a mysterious man he had taken prisoner, showing an island with a cross indicating a hidden treasure; that later he sailed along the coast of Nova Scotia several times; and that he was notorious for burying his booty where it could not be found. Some scholars unite the two theories, based on the possible relationship of the famous pirate to the Order of the Temple. If this link is true, then the possessor of the map was also a Templar who entrusted it to Kidd, following orders from a superior. What was the purpose? Perhaps because Captain Kidd would then be obliged to add part of his spoils to the hidden riches of the Order, or perhaps simply because this would ensure that the Great Secret would remain in its hiding place.

Less believable is the theory that the well dates from the eighteenth century, and that it contains the crown jewels of France. These jewels disappeared in 1771, and it is said that they were sold as contraband in French Canada, more precisely at Louisbourg, a town on Cape Breton. Since the town suffered frequent English attacks, the jewels were moved to nearby Oak Island and hidden in the now famous well. Another version, which has proved completely absurd, holds that the well contains the works of William Shakespeare, which Francis Bacon had hidden there in the seventeenth century (with what intent is not known). In spite of one treasure hunter claiming to have found a trove of these originals, they have never been displayed, and literary history firmly denies this possibility. However, it should not be forgotten that Francis Bacon was also a Templar.

What the disappointed treasure hunters did find was immense difficulty in reaching the bottom of the well. Besides the well's depth (it was excavated down to fifty meters, somewhat less than half the estimated total), each attempt has been thwarted by all kinds of obstacles and a current of subterranean water, diverted in order to prevent access to the lower levels. In one of the first attempts, a great stone was encountered that blocked the passage, on whose reverse the following inscription was engraved:

∇ ⧖·\ØΔ∠ =   ∇⁚⁚Δ =   ⊤⁚⊏\⧠ =
Δⵔ\ =   ⊬⸱'⸱⊏⊏⸱'⸱\⤬ =
⊖\+⤬ⵔ☉ =   ·Ø⁚ =   ⊤+Ø⸱'⸱⁚ⵔ =

There are various interpretations for this, but the most believable is:

"FORTY FEET BELOW TWO MILLION POUNDS ARE BURIED."

8

THE MYSTERY
OF CHRISTOPHER
COLUMBUS

The figure of Christopher Columbus, where he came from, the reason for his voyages, and his strange behavior have all been fodder for enduring disagreements among historians, some belonging to various countries or municipalities vying for the honor of having been his origin. Hardly any of them still accept the childish fable clung to by conservative academics and persistently taught in schools.

This story relates that Columbus was a Genoese mariner of humble origin who claimed that the earth was round while ignorant scholars believed it was flat. He offered to prove it was round by sailing to India in the reverse direction—that is, going west. The Catholic monarchs agreed to sponsor Columbus's idea, and Isabella pawned her jewels to finance the great adventure, which resulted in the "discovery of America." According to this classroom version, Columbus died poor and forgotten, ignorant of the greatness of his deed.

Almost all these claims are false, even within the facts established and confirmed by the academic community. The enlightened Greeks and Romans, not to mention medieval astrologers, already knew or guessed that the earth was round, and this knowledge was widespread among educated people in the fifteenth century, especially among astronomers, navigators, and cartographers—so Columbus had nothing to prove in this regard. Also, people at this time were already toying with the

125

idea of reaching the Indies and China by sailing to the west, above all because the Portuguese had expanded their navigation throughout the Atlantic. However, sailors' stories claimed that beyond the Azores there was a vast ocean populated by monstrous creatures and ravaged by terrible storms, which made it difficult to recruit crews willing to confront these fantastic perils. Reverting to historical revisionism, we can say that Columbus was probably not a Genoese mariner from a humble family, that the expedition was not financed by the queen's jewels, and that the "discoverer" knew exactly where he was going—and perhaps had even been there before.

For their part, numerous scholars of secret societies and occult mysteries in the undercurrents of historical facts claim outright that no one knows who Christopher Columbus really was, that this name was an occultist alias, that he did not speak a word of Italian, that he may have been a French pirate, a Jewish cartographer, or one of the late Cathars— and even that all these qualities might have been split between two distinct people who had some kind of agreement. At any rate, as mentioned in the previous chapter, he was certainly not the first European to reach the New World.

Some of the questions asked by scholars about the personality and history of Christopher Columbus are:

- How did the son of a humble Genoese family receive a high education, mingling with the aristocracy in such class-ridden societies as those of Portugal and Spain in the fifteenth century?
- How was a sailor with neither title nor fortune able to marry a young Portuguese woman of high lineage?
- Why did Columbus originally present himself as Colombo, which in Italian means "dove," symbol of the Holy Ghost, often present in the symbolism of the Order of the Knights of the Temple?
- If, according to his contemporaries, he spoke hardly any Italian, could he have been the French pirate of the same era who was called Colomba (dove in French)?
- Why did he choose to decorate the sails of his caravels with the open-armed cross of the Templars?

- Is it merely a coincidence that Columbus's first expedition weighed anchor on August 3, 1492, two days after the deadline of the edict expelling the Jews from Spain?
- Why were his men willing to face the legendary perils of the ocean?
- Was the crew formed of exiled Jews who had no other option, and were his captains members of the Order of the Temple?
- Why were his voyages financed by Jewish bankers, as has been historically confirmed?
- Why did Columbus bring no priests on his first voyage, as was the practice on all maritime expeditions to the East Indies and Africa?
- If he thought he had reached a powerful and rich Hindustani land, or maybe Cathay, the magnificent empire of the Great Khan, then why did he take possession of these lands in the name of Spain?
- Is it true that prominent figures in the twentieth century, such as Franklin D. Roosevelt and Charles de Gaulle, made important political decisions dictated by secret documents from this distant time?

Christopher Columbus explaining his project in the monastery of Rábida. (Painting by Vázquez Díaz in the same monastery.)

To find some answers to these questions, we must return to the place and time in which those events took place.

Kings and Navigators

The effect of Spain's discovery of a New World unjustly minimized the decisive importance of Portugal in the so-called age of discoveries. In truth, Portugal contributed to the knowledge of the world more than any other nation, including Spain, and the story relates once again to the Order of the Temple. At the beginning of the fourteenth century, the fugitive Templar ships of La Rochelle took three different routes in search of refuge. As we have said, one flotilla was received by Robert the Bruce, liberator of Scotland, and another by the Norman monarch of Sicily, Roger II. The third headed for Portugal, ruled by King Dionisio the Liberal, also called Don Diniz and nicknamed O Lavrador, "the farmer," for his dedication to promoting agriculture. (Certain scholars point out the similarity of this name to that of the coast of Labrador, the first American land explored by Europeans.) This benevolent sovereign also belonged to the Order of the Temple, whose presence in Portugal went back to certain episodes in the twelfth century.

In 1147, King Alfonso Enriquez completed his campaign against the Moors and entered Lisbon triumphantly to be crowned. The Templars, then at the height of their prestige, had fought on his side at the decisive battle of Ourique. The Order of the Temple stayed with the sovereign to defend his new frontiers while the Cistercians devoted themselves to eradicating Muslim influence from the faith of his subjects. Despite being a very cultured monarch for his time, Alfonso, probably against the wishes of the Temple and the Cistercians, expelled the Muslims and Jews from Portugal for reasons of security. To fill the resulting void in mercantile activities, many Genoese merchants and bankers arrived (some of them clandestine Jews), and their descendants financed maritime expeditions and the exploration of new territories three centuries later.

The Templars, always fond of architecture, built numerous castles, monasteries, and churches in Portugal, especially in the city of Tomar, in the Santarém District north of Lisbon. (This area has retained a legendary aura from the time of Hercules; in 1912 the Virgin Mary appeared there, in the town of Fátima.) The Order of the Temple set up a central seat and base of operations there, building many edifices in typical Templar styles. The most prominent was the Church of Santa Maria do Olivar, with a round base like the Holy Sepulchre in Jerusalem. Another notable structure built for the Temple was the nearby church of Saint Gregory, with an octagonal ground plan, like all those dedicated to this third-century thaumaturge bishop. When the Order was excommunicated and banned, the king of Portugal maintained his kingdom's traditional loyalty to the Templars and they founded a new order, the Knights of Christ, as a cover. In order to better protect this order, they chose the king as their Grand Master. The new pope, John XXII, agreed to consecrate the order of King Don Diniz, and gave his spiritual guidance to the order of the Cistercian monks; it is not known whether he was aware of the traditional complicity between these two orders.

The most distinguished Grand Master of the revived Order of the Temple in Portugal was Prince Henry the Navigator, who had little chance of becoming king since he was the third son of Manuel I. He dedicated himself fervently to navigation and naval war, conquering the African city of Ceuta in 1415. This victory gave him the idea of exploring the African coast, using some of the immense capital that the Templars possessed. He founded a nautical school in Sagres near the Cape of Saint Vincent, where he met with mariners and cartographers to study the ancient maps that formed part of the legacy of the Temple. Some, of Phoenician origin, showed regions of the African coast unknown to European geographers. Henry eventually gave up seafaring, but continued his studies in Sagres, promoting numerous expeditions until his death in 1460. He encouraged the navigators who reached the Indian Ocean by sea, and doubtless partially inspired Christopher Columbus's voyages to the New World.

It now remains for us to find the reasons why Columbus came to Portugal. The latest available historical data allow us to trace an approximate outline of his youth, beginning by accepting that he was born in 1451 and indeed came from a Genoese family, though not a poor one. His father owned a large cloth factory and his mother carried on a lucrative cheese trade. Several chronicles assert that he did not speak Italian,

Sailors of Palos, de Moguer, the city from which Columbus sailed, were fearful of an expedition whose goal they did not know. (Painting by Vázquez Díaz in the monastery of Rábida.)

and they could be right, because the young Christopher would have grown up speaking the Genoese dialect, quite different from the Italian of Rome, and took to the seas while still an adolescent. At the age of eighteen, he entered into the service of the French pirate Guillaume de Casenove, who harassed Atlantic merchants between Venice and Flanders. One document suggests that Columbus was one of the French corsairs who, according to the chronicles, attacked the coasts of Valencia and Catalonia in 1473. Later on, he took part in a battle between the Genoese and the Turks over the rich mastic-producing Aegean island of Chios, and finally embarked on a merchant convoy from Genoa that carried gum from Chios to the ports of England, Portugal, and France. Columbus's ship was attacked and sunk by this same pirate Casenove, but he managed to save himself from the shipwreck and swim to the Portuguese coast. In Lisbon, the influential Genoese community of the city welcomed him, and it was possibly here that he made his first contact with the Temple.

A Happy Marriage

The young sailor was about twenty-five years old, good-looking and courteous, and he had a rare talent for enthralling women with illusionist games and tales of pirates, shipwrecks, and mysterious islands. These qualities attracted the young Felipa Perestrello e Moniz, the daughter of a well-to-do and prestigious Lisboan family, and the two were married in 1479. Felipa was a descendant of Bartolomeu Perestrello, a mariner of Genoese origin belonging to the Temple, who had worked with Henry the Navigator in the school at Sagres. In 1419 the prince had sent for Perestrello, together with the Templar navigators Tristán Vaz Teixeira and João Gonçalvez Zarco, to conquer the Madeira archipelago off northwest Africa. The three knights were awarded the title of *capitano,* which implied the rank of hereditary governors of the islands. The government of the island of Porto Santo was assigned to the Perestrello family.

The great windfall for the fortune of the Madeira settlers was sugar. This was a traditional crop of India, where it was called *sakkara* in Sanskrit. The Arab merchants called it *sukkar* and imported it to Europe,

traversing a long and hazardous route by land and sea. The settlers Perestrello brought to the island planted sugarcane, with such good results
that they soon began exporting it to Flanders, England, and Venice. The
dark side of this prosperity was the use of African slaves in harvesting
the crop.

In the first half-century of Portuguese colonization of Madeira, no
fewer than eight hundred families landed on the various islands, among
them some who came from Scotland. One of the first Scottish colonists
was a nephew of Henry Sinclair, whose daughter Elizabeth had married John Drummond, a member of another powerful Scottish clan, very
closely linked to the Order of the Temple. His son of the same name
was the husband of Catarina Vaz de Lordelo, widow of a member of
the Perestrello family; later, the Scottish pioneer married Branca Afonso
da Cunha, by whom he had nine daughters and sons. They and their
descendants married various members of the Perestrello family, so that
in Madeira the two clans behaved as one.

Upon arrival in Lisbon, Columbus connected with a relative (possibly
one of his brothers) who ran a shop selling maps and marine charts. This
business was not far from the Church of the Monastery of All Saints, where,
during Mass, the young Christopher and Felipa Perestrello exchanged their
first glances. Perhaps the first conversation between the two was about the
common origin of their families in Piacenza, one of the reasons they used
to explain why such an unequal courtship quickly followed. Columbus's
parents, although they were neither rich nor of grand lineage, had commercial relations with important families of Piacenza, and some friendships among them. Besides the fact that Felipa had fallen in love with the
personal qualities of the young mariner, there were three other reasons
that inclined the Perestrello family to accept the marriage: Christopher
was one of their countrymen, which inspired a certain confidence then,
just as it does today; he had precocious and extensive nautical experience,
always an asset for a family of navigators; and above all, he was a member
of the Order of the Temple, or at least was inclined to join it.

After the wedding, Christopher and Felipa moved to Porto Santo,
governed by her elder brother after the death of her father, Bartolomeu.
Columbus's mother-in-law then gave him an invaluable gift: the maps,
documents, and diaries of her late husband, and the possibility of spend-

ing as much time as he wanted reading and studying in the library of one of the first great Portuguese expeditionary navigators. Christopher did not waste this opportunity. Without doubt, his father-in-law had written down the oral histories that circulated in Madeira about the mysterious islands to the west, and he had inherited documents on the travels of Henry Sinclair, if not the actual accounts of the voyage and the marine maps drawn by the Zeno brothers. It is impossible to establish how much documentation Perestrello had regarding the Hermetic knowledge held by the Templars of ancient voyages and landings in the New World, but it may have gone back to the Phoenicians and Egyptians, and even as far as the myth of Atlantis itself.

Other volumes Columbus must have read include Greek and Roman works, such as those of Pliny, Strabo, and Marinus of Tyre. This last divided the world into twenty-four "hours" of distance, and Columbus was able to calculate that there were eight of these hours between the recently discovered Cape Verde Islands and the coast of Asia. Strabo, the Greek geographer of the first century BC, stated that Asia could be reached by crossing the Atlantic, something also believed by Aristotle and Seneca. The third-century Roman Gaius Julius Solinus had already spoken of the "Indies," which could be reached by sailing for forty days past the Gorgon islands (Cape Verde, off the coast of Senegal). Finally, Aristotle also claimed the existence of a "sea of codfish" near a fertile island in the middle of the ocean; at least he was right about the fish. Columbus, at a time when printing had recently been invented, was an insatiable reader. It is said that his favorite book was the *Imago Mundi,* by the French geographer Pierre d'Ailly, which assumed the terrestrial globe to be round, maintained that the earth rotated on its axis, and estimated distances in the Atlantic. It is very probable that Columbus also read Seneca's *Medea,* which contains a prophecy announcing that this ocean would one day be crossed.

With all this information available, the future "discoverer" began to envision great possibilities in sailing to the west. The Knights of Christ— that is, the Templars of Portugal—had obtained maps that their king, Alfonso V, had kept with the Florentine cosmographer Paolo dal Pozzo Toscanelli. Columbus gained access to these in 1480, and verified that in 1474 Toscanelli had proposed to the Portuguese monarch a shorter and more direct route to Cipango, the name given to Japan in the chronicles of Marco Polo. Columbus immediately began a correspondence with the Florentine, and it is said that he obtained much information and a mysterious map of the Atlantic from Toscanelli. In 1482, Columbus joined the expedition of Diego de Azambuja, sent by the Portuguese Crown to explore the Gold Coast of Africa; this allowed him to test the performance of his ships on long oceanic voyages. Two years later, he finally decided to make a voyage westward across the Atlantic.

A Time of Setbacks

By marrying a Portuguese woman, Christopher Columbus had become a subject of that kingdom, and so he submitted his plan to King João II. The sovereign sent him on to the Naval Council, which, without passing judgment on his theory, determined that his plan was inappropriate. At the time, Portugal was putting all its efforts into expeditions seeking to reach India by going around Africa, thus avoiding the menace of the Turks. By contrast, the admirals and cartographers who made up the council knew there was a large unexplored island between Europe and Asia, or maybe a whole continent, and they were surprised by Columbus's ignorance. Why did the navigator hide his knowledge? Perhaps because he feared that the learned men would consider the idea of exploring those unknown lands too risky and of doubtful benefit. At this time, all of Europe was obsessed with the riches of Asia, and its monarchs wanted to find the quickest and safest route to reach India, Cathay, and remote Cipango. The experts who advised them knew that the best route was not across the Atlantic, as Columbus must also have known.

Why did he not turn to the Temple, whose immense riches would have easily permitted the financing of the expedition? For one thing, the true relationship between Columbus and the Templar order is not known, nor do we know whether the Templars wanted him to be the one to rediscover the New World at this time. The Templars were powerful but not omnipotent, and had to move forward with their plans slowly so as not to go against the priorities and strategies of political powers. Nevertheless, João II, who as king of Portugal must have also been the Grand Master of the Knights of Christ, sent a caravel to explore the ocean without the knowledge of the Maritime Council. When this

It is said that Columbus took water for his historical voyage from the spring of Roman origin known as La Fontanilla, located at the entrance to Palos, de Moguer.

expedition returned empty handed, the sovereign put the project on the back shelf.

Columbus then had a new setback to deal with: Felipa died suddenly at their house in Madeira. Her elder brother inherited all the titles and fortune of the Perestrello family, without offering anything to the distraught widower. For this reason, relations became icy between Columbus and his brother-in-law, who treated him like an intruder in the lofty family. Columbus left Madeira with resentment, and soon afterward left Portugal for Spain, the other great maritime power of the era.

There, he came into contact with Friar Juan Pérez, prior of the convent of La Rábida and the queen's confessor, who transmitted Columbus's petition for an audience to the queen. Time passed with no response, but the Franciscan friar's monastic brother Friar Antonio de Marchena became interested in the project. Marchena was a recognized cosmographer, and he brought Columbus various maps and pieces of information in his possession. However, the royal palace maintained an irritating silence, despite Friar Pérez's knowledge that the king and queen were aware of Columbus's presence in Spain and the general outline of his project. Then the royal clerk entered the scene: Luis de Santángel, an influential converted Jew who, together with the treasurer to the Crown, Alonso de Quintanilla, succeeded in having an advisory council in Cordoba listen to Columbus.

It is unlikely that the Genovese navigator gave the famous demonstration of the egg before the advisers, or that he discussed with them whether the earth was flat or round. According to them, he insisted that he hoped to reach Asia, presented the arguments in favor of his plan, and related the great benefits that his expedition would bring to Castile. The council did not give an immediate response, although they must have passed on their opinion to the Catholic monarchs. Ferdinand and Isabella were too occupied with the final stages of the siege of Granada, completing what is known as the Reconquest of Spain by removing the last Muslim bastion. They kept silent for two long years. During this time Columbus tried once more to convince King João II, but unfortunately for him, the news had just arrived in Lisbon that Portuguese navigators had rounded the southern tip of Africa via the Cape of Good Hope, opening up a new route to the Orient by way of the Indian Ocean. João II had spent a fortune on these expeditions, and was not interested in going into debt in search of new uncertain routes, or in finding an alleged far-off and unknown Atlantic continent.

Columbus and the Promised Land

Meanwhile, Columbus's contacts in Genoa had convinced the rich Jewish banker Francesco Pinello that financing the voyage across the Atlantic would be an excellent investment—not only for the presumed riches of the new lands, but because thousands of Jewish families could settle there as colonists, safe from constant persecution. Jewish communities in Europe continued to dream of the return to Eretz Israel, and promised each year in their Pesach festival (Passover) that next year they would celebrate in Jerusalem. But the discriminations, humiliations, killings, and expulsions that they suffered throughout almost all of Europe made it a priority for them to realize this symbolic desire as soon as possible. Some Jewish leaders had gone to the Ottoman Empire to ask that a piece of the biblical Promised Land be ceded to them for this purpose, offering in exchange a considerable monetary compensation. The offer was not unreasonable, since the Turks showed much more tolerance than the Europeans for the numerous Jewish communities that lived and prospered in their territory. However, Sultan Mehmet II refused to sell them this part of Palestine, perhaps out of fear that the proposal was a stratagem devised by the European kings with whom he was at war.

The Jewish leaders then resolved that their Promised Land could be any place where their people could live in peace and build a "New Jerusalem." This idea coincided, both in scope and in objective, with the millenary mission undertaken by the Priory of Sion and the Order of the Temple. In both cases, the essential object was to find a place to build a new, different, and better society. The fact that for the Jews it was the refuge of a persecuted people and for the Templars a millenary and universal project was a difference in the ends that did not prevent sharing the means. There is much information that demonstrates a strong link between the Order of the Temple and the Hermetic knowledge of the ancient Hebrews, going back to the time of the Order's foundation in the Holy Land. Both societies shared a great veneration for the Temple of Solomon, and both carefully guarded the testimonies of ancestral knowledge.

At the end of the fifteenth century, Jews and Templars were two communities that had been persecuted for a long time by the Vatican and the Christian kingdoms. It is not surprising that they united to help each other, even without the connections they may have maintained before then. This complicity may have propelled and financed Christopher Columbus's Atlantic crossing, considering that both Jews and Templars held great riches and secret influence over all the monarchs of Europe (and the Holy See?). It appears indubitable that Pinello and other Jewish bankers of Genoa brought together a considerable sum of money that they sent to their agents in Spain, the converts Diego de Deza and Gabriel Sánchez. Santángel then had an audience with Isabella, who was more inclined than her husband to sponsor the voyage under the flag of Castile and Aragon. It is unlikely that the Genoese bankers persuaded the queen to deposit her jewels as collateral, as the legend relates—above all because she had no lack of money, and also because this was not technically a loan, but rather an investment.

The Queen's Jewels

An anonymous and little-known story, perhaps from some member of the court who aspired to be a chronicler, tells an anecdote that may have given rise to the myth that Isabella pawned her jewels to buy Columbus his ships. According to this account, King Ferdinand was much more reticent about the project than his wife, probably because it would require some of the Crown's treasure. It describes the scene in which Santángel appeared before the queen with a coffer and said:

"Madame, here is the money for the expedition. I cannot say where it came from, and I beg you keep the secret."

"But . . . what shall I tell the king?"

"Tell him, your majesty, that you have pawned your jewels."

At this point we cannot avoid the controversial question of whether Christopher Columbus, as well as being a Templar, was a Jew. If so, he was the ideal candidate for undertaking a joint enterprise of the Order of the Temple and Judaism, especially considering his nautical knowledge and personal determination. The Spanish author Salvador de Madariaga, in his *Vida del muy magnífico señor don Cristóbal Colón*, proposes the theory that Columbus was a Jew. He claims that the Colom family were Catalan Jews who had settled in Genoa, and that in the family they continued to speak their language (which, together with the Genoese dialect and port jargon, explains the navigator's peculiar oral and written expression). He adds that Columbus was a rootless man who did not remain faithful to the monarchs he served, and that he was a glutton. He appears to attribute these characteristics to all Jews, and only to them.

Although Madariaga reveals more prejudice than documentation in his work; his publication motivated more serious research and investigation regarding the possible Jewish origin of Christopher Columbus. Those who defend the idea that he was Jewish point out the fact that Columbus always offered confusing stories about his origin, and that he had very probably changed his first name (no Jew would have been called Christopher) and almost certainly his surname as well. They also point out that the textile trade in fifteenth-century Genoa was almost exclusively in the hands of Jews, and that Columbus's strange signature was a Kabbalistic symbol. As has been mentioned, he brought no missionary friar on his first voyage, in spite of the aid he had received from the Franciscans. But the main argument of these scholars in favor of Columbus's Jewish origin is the financing of his voyage by the bankers of the Jewish community in Genoa. Would they have placed a gentile at the head of their expedition to the Promised Land?

The Return of the Templars

From the point of view of this book, it is irrelevant whether or not Columbus was a Jew, but it is relevant whether or not he was a Templar. It is known that the Order of the Temple accepted converts of Jewish origin, and even accepted Muslim informers and collaborators. Some documents about Columbus, and others in his own handwriting, give fuel to the idea that he belonged to some type of secret society or sect. It is known that the money received from Genoa bought three caravels, whose names are famous: the *Santa Maria,* the *Pinta,* and the *Nina.* The first was commanded by Columbus himself, and the other two by the brothers Martín Alonso and Vicente Yánez Pinzón, who were Templars, or at least answered to them. According to certain chronicles, at least one of them had already visited the New World on expeditions of exploration or piracy sponsored by the Temple. We should remember that the young Columbus had also been a pirate, a profession always linked in various ways to the Templar order.

It has always been believed, probably with good reason, that the name of the flagship *Santa Maria* was in homage to the Virgin Mary, to whom Isabella was greatly devoted. But it is also possible that under this pretext, Columbus wanted to honor Mary Magdalene, the chief saint of the Templars, for having carried the Royal Blood in her womb. Martín Pinzón had a caravel named the *Pinta* because in the past this name had brought him good luck. His younger brother chose a ship of smaller size, the *Santa Clara,* perhaps because this name reminded him of the industrious Templar navigator Henry Sinclair, or Saint Clair. But later he decided to rechristen it the *Nina* ("girl"), perhaps at Columbus's indication. Historians explain that he gave it this name because it was the smallest of the three caravels, but scholars of Hermetic Christology have other explanations. If the *Santa Maria* was Mary Magdalene, the *Nina* accompanying her could be none other than her daughter, the mythical Sarah who continued the lineage of Jesus. The cryptic symbolic message of the caravels, then, was that Mary Magdalene took the sacred child to a New World so that the Royal Blood could flourish there.

It is not worth repeating the known vicissitudes of Christopher Columbus's four voyages to what we now call America, which he knew was not India or Cathay. Had he believed he would reach these rich lands of the Orient, he would have brought European merchandise on board to exchange for costly silk and spices. But the caravels carried only a few cases of colorful hats, glass beads, metal bells, and other trinkets, sufficient to impress semi-savage natives but not, at that time, such a personage as the Great Khan. As we have said, Columbus was not seeking new mercantile routes but instead an appropriate place for building the New Jerusalem.

Why, then, did he take possession of these lands in the name of the Catholic monarchs? In this era it was impossible for a private society or religious order (least of all a secret society) to conquer and colonize new territories. Only the European and Christian crowns could take possession of a "land of heretics," and the disputes among them were subject to the arbitration of Our Most Holy Lord, the pope (as Alexander VI called himself in 1493 in his bull *Inter caetera,* which set the first limits between Spanish and Portuguese possessions). The Order of the Temple was also banned, excommunicated, and persecuted, and its members acted in the strictest secrecy. Therefore, they needed a European kingdom that would serve as a cover for their purpose in the New World—and what better cover than the most Catholic of sovereigns, Isabella and Ferdinand?

9

IN SEARCH
OF NEW ARCADIA

A Templar tradition holds that Henry Sinclair, on his pre-Columbian voyage to America, founded a colony where Newport, Rhode Island, is today. As the reader already knows, Sinclair's final objective was to build Arcadia, or New Jerusalem, the longed-for holy and perfect city of ancestral mythology. Two centuries later, in 1524, the Florentine navigator and explorer Giovanni da Verrazano went on a voyage with the purpose of making contact with the possible descendants of those earlier colonists.

Verrazano, born in 1485, came from a noble Florentine family whose castle in Val di Greve had been built upon Roman ruins, which in their turn had been built on an Etruscan settlement from the sixth century BC. The Verrazano ancestry did not go back that far, but was old enough that the family guarded knowledge obtained from the secret societies of the High Middle Ages. Perhaps their ancestors had maintained contact with the Priory of Sion or had been involved in the ups and downs of the Templar knights. This mysterious tradition did not impede Giovanni's interest in the new discoveries and innovative ideas of the Renaissance, especially the enigmas and challenges presented by the New World. It should be remembered that Florence was the center of Italian politics and Renaissance art; the future explorer was a contemporary and countryman of such fascinating characters as the Medici family and the brilliant, mysterious Leonardo da Vinci.

Porcelain plate with the arms of Florence.

Another element to note is that the patron saint of Florence was John the Baptist, the Essene prophet, inspirer of the Gnostics and teacher of Jesus of Nazareth. The city of the Medici and the Verrazano had been a refuge in the thirteenth century for the Lombard Cathars persecuted in the bloody crusade of Simon de Montfort. More than two centuries later, their religion had still not been extinguished, and many Florentines practiced it surreptitiously, adding the Gnostic traditions that had been brought along the Silk Route from places in the Levant. This background of secret sects and Christian esotericism was concealed from the official Catholicism of the city, whose rulers were powerful enough to choose who the new pope would be, sometimes putting a member of their family in the place of a deceased pontiff, as Lorenzo the Magnificent did for his son Giovanni, who took the name Leo X.

In 1453, an enigmatic document entitled *Habeas Hermeticum* arrived in Florence, probably from the secret Order of the Temple. The text was said to have been written by Hermes Trismegistus, the Greek name of the Egyptian god Thoth, creator of the arts and sciences. This document, which was not divine but was indeed very ancient, had been used by the dissident sects of the first centuries of Christianity, and its clandestine circulation among the Florentines revived their interest in ancestral sources. At the end of the fifteenth century, the long arm of the Inquisition reached liberal and esoteric Florence in the person of the implacable monk Girolamo Savonarola. The Verrazano family, whose escutcheon bore a Gnostic star with six points, quickly changed it to eight points, the occultist significance of which was unknown to the Dominican inquisitors. In spite of this precaution, many Verrazanos decided to leave the city, among them Giovanni, who was about fifteen years old at the time.

Perhaps accompanied by one or more relatives, the young Verrazano arrived in Lyon to live in exile. This southern French city was, at the time, both a bastion of traditional Catholicism and a historical center for the sects that questioned it. Some bishops of Lyon had become famous for their furious fights with the Cathars and the sizable Jewish community of the region. The city had also been a ritual center for the worshippers of Cybele, the Great Goddess or Mother of the Gods of the cults of Mesopotamia, corresponding to the Black Virgin in Templar rituals. This deity was highly venerated in Rome until Constantine imposed Christianity, and she was still worshipped in Lyon for a century afterward. The Roman Vestals slaughtered a bull as a sacrifice to the goddess, and when the Temple of Cybele in Lyon was replaced by the basilica of Notre-Dame de Fourvière, Lyonnaise maidens continued to sacrifice rams and cockerels in honor of the Black Virgin.

Giovanni da Verrazano studied and grew to manhood in this city of underlying paganism, where Cathars, Templars, and Huguenots still maintained their hidden presence. Perhaps he chose to live there because the city had something in common with Florence: Both had been seats of the Gnostic knowledge reclaimed by the Cathars, and both were important textile centers linked with the routes of Asia.

The Templar Port

An older brother of Giovanni married into the Guadagni, another suspicious patrician family that had been expelled from Italy around 1505, its more prominent members taking refuge in France. Giovanni and his brother Girolamo moved to the port of Dieppe, in Normandy, where their brother-in-law chartered ships that sailed the Silk Route.

The third important city in Verrazano's life boasted an ancient

Although he accepted baptism only on his deathbed, Constantine is considered the first Christian emperor. (Fourteenth-century mosaic, Museum of Saint Mark, Venice.)

maritime tradition and played an important role at the time in the new expeditions spurred by the "discovery" of the West Indies. Before this event, in 1362, Dieppe's navigators had reached the coast of Sierra Leone, in Africa, and established a colonial enclave there called Petit Dieppe; and Jean Cousin, the captain whose ship was blown off course by a tempest to the coast of Brazil in 1488, four years before Columbus's first voyage, had also sailed from this port.

In fact, the entire coast of Normandy had been France's maritime base since it was conquered by the Viking chief Rollo, ancestor of the familiar Henry Sinclair. The Church of Saint-Jacques in Dieppe was famous for having actually been a sanctuary of the Temple. This enormous cathedral boasts twenty chapels, one of them in octagonal form, as well as rose windows, flying buttresses, strange gargoyles, and other elements characteristic of the Templar-style.

When Francis I came to the throne of France in 1515, he not only imported the artistic ideas and concepts of the Renaissance from Italy, but was also resolved to participate in the maritime race to discover and explore new oceanic routes. To this end, he sent for the most important man in Dieppe, the rich merchant and ship owner Jean d'Ango, who had been a pirate in his time and had managed to become to France what Henry the Navigator was to Portugal. Girolamo da Verrazano, who had a connection to d'Ango for commercial and social reasons, presented his younger brother to the shipping magnate. Giovanni, who had an inclination to seafaring and had taken several voyages in order to learn the arts of the sea, dreamed of one day going on a fantastic expedition to the Indies. It is also probable that Girolamo and d'Ango knew of the voyage of Henry Sinclair. In this case, it would have inspired the young mariner to go off in search of the colony that, according to the Zeno brothers, Sinclair had established in some marvelous lands to the south of Newfoundland. This project coincided with the expeditionary ambitions of Francis I, and this fortunate coincidence encouraged its realization.

By now, the Kingdom of France had already achieved a maritime capacity very close to that boasted by Spain and Portugal. The navigators of Dieppe had passed the Cape of Good Hope and visited the islands of Sumatra and Java. Relations between Francis I and Charles V were very tense, and his ships had ongoing scuffles with the imperial fleet. When d'Ango proposed this voyage to the unexplored coasts of North America, the French king saw the great possibility of acquiring vast extensions to his kingdom and finally finding the passage to the Orient via the Pacific. These achievements might make France into the greatest maritime power of all time.

After d'Ango persuaded Francis I to receive Giovanni da Verrazano, the latter appeared before the monarch with a long poem, which he began to read in a high voice. This was *Arcadia,* by the Neapolitan poet Jacopo Sannazaro, exiled in France. The work is a complex composition in verse and prose, combining the legend of the idyllic paradise of ancestral folklore with the arcane mysteries of secret sects. The poem has various levels of interpretation, some of which reveal esoteric messages to the initiated. Giovanni explained to the monarch that Sannazaro defended the existence of Arcadia, but that he did not locate it in Greece, placing it instead on the other side of the Atlantic Ocean.

Perhaps Francis I saw this mythical land as a symbol of his future possessions, or maybe it only proved Verrazano's eagerness to find out everything relating to the New World. But what is certain is that the king gave his approval for the voyage, which was financed by the magnates of the Silk Route.

The Voyage to Arcadia

Scholars disagree about the scant and confusing information regarding the first stage of Verrazano's voyage. It is known that the Florentine navigator sailed from Dieppe with four ships chartered by the Crown in the autumn of 1523. However, only one ship completed the transatlantic voyage, supposedly because two of the others set off to practice piracy upon Spanish merchants and a third had to return home, dismasted in a tempest. In his previous voyages, Verrazano had been to Portugal and its colonial enclave Mozambique, so he had good relations with the Portuguese admiralty. He was thus able to obtain authorization to make his first stop at Madeira, the island that had been conquered by Portugal and ruled by Columbus's father-in-law, and where Columbus had received very valuable information for his famous undertaking.

As has been explained, Columbus was Genoese, and was therefore accepted by the Genoese community of Madeira. But in this era there was no standardized Italian language, and the Genoese, although they understood the language Verrazano spoke, would have considered him a foreigner, sailing under the French flag to boot. For this reason, it is unlikely that the Florentine was well received by the rich Genoese bourgeoisie of the island, and more likely that he used his connections with the Knights of Christ—that is, the Templar colonists descended from the

Sinclair clan. In any case, in his report to Francis I, Verrazano reported only that he stopped at a "desert islet," which may well have been the small and almost uninhabited island of Porto Santo, governed by the Templar family of Felipa de Perestrello, Columbus's Portuguese wife.

Giovanni da Verrazano left Madeira on January 17, 1524, on board a single ship christened the *Dauphin* in homage to the prince of France. His brother Girolamo accompanied him as cartographer, and the crew consisted of fifty men. The ship had provisions for eight months at sea. The *Dauphin* set sail westward, and after some forty days, Verrazano sighted the coast of what is now North Carolina, near Cape Hatteras— but they had to change course to the north upon sighting a Spanish squadron. The explorer gave Florentine names to the points on the coast that his brother described, such as Annunziata, Francesca, and even Verrazania. Later he translated them into French in the diary of the voyage that he wrote for the king. None of these place-names is preserved today, but they were presumably located between the Pamlico estuary and Delaware Bay.

The *Dauphin* continued northward until entering what is now New York Bay, and, following the same course, arrived at Manhattan Island, near the strait that is still known as the Verrazano Narrows. The explorer christened the whole bay Santa Margarita, in honor of King Francis's sister, the duchess of Alençon. The explorers continued around Long Island and explored another island that they called Rhodes, because of its bucolic scenery similar to that described in Sannazaro's poem about the Greek island of that name. Today, this region is the state of Rhode Island. There they made contact with the Wampanoag tribe, part of the Algonquin Nation. According to Verrazano's diary, the natives were not surprised to see them, and some of them even seemed to be trying to imitate the clothing of Europeans with their skins and feathers. He described them as a community that practiced chastity and monogamy, as well as charity toward the weaker or less fortunate members of the tribe. It was the Wampanoag who informed the navigator that a "sacred building" had been constructed at the end of what is now Newport Bay.

They sailed for this location, and to their surprise and joy they saw a baptistery of indubitable Templar-style standing by the coast. Verrazano took note of its location and other details, while Girolamo located it on his map and made a rough sketch of its architecture. This structure, although made of local materials, presented a clear similarity in form and size to the constructions of the Cistercians and the Templars in Europe in the Low Middle Ages. The place was empty, and there were few signs of human presence in the surrounding area, suggesting that the builders had not stayed. On Verrazano's map, this site is marked "Norman Villa," revealing half its secret but concealing from the profane its true character and significance.

The expedition continued by sea to Newfoundland, and from there returned to the port of Dieppe, where they arrived at the beginning of July of the same year, 1524. The great success of Verrazano's secret mission was publicly a failure. They had not found the hoped-for passage to the Pacific, and in fact had not even looked for it. Their exploration of virgin territories was not of interest to Francis I, who was occupied with a disastrous war against the empire, ending the next year with the capture of the French monarch at the battle of Pavia. As for the precise map of the Atlantic coast drawn up by Girolamo, it was of no use to his patrons, who were dealing in Oriental silk.

Death in the Caribbean

A few years afterward, Giovanni da Verrazano went on another voyage to the Americas, aiming to restore his damaged prestige. This time he sailed for the West Indies, perhaps to dispute the possession of some of the islands there with the Spaniards. He dropped anchor on the coast of Guadalupe and, leaving his men on board, went ashore alone. There he was received by the natives with whom he wanted to converse. But the Caribs were not peaceful like the Wampanoags; yelling ferociously, they seized the navigator and took him away by force. From the anchored ship, the terrified crewmen watched the cannibals roast their captain in the style of the buccaneers, and eat him bit by bit.

The Signs of the Temple

Ten years after Verrazano's unsuccessful return, Francis I again started to contemplate searching for a shorter route to Cathay and taking possession of the northern lands of America. Free from his imprisonment after signing the treaty of Cambray, he prepared a new attack on Emperor Charles V, with the complicity of the Protestant German princes. Perhaps to pray for the success of this future enterprise, he made a private pilgrimage to the sanctuary of Mont-Saint-Michel. There he connected with another pilgrim, the expert mariner Jacques Cartier, native of the port of Saint-Malo. Cartier had closely studied Verrazano's maps and writings, with which the king was obviously also familiar. The navigator expressed his suspicion that the Florentine explorers had seen more things than they had told of in the diary of their voyage—perhaps silver or gold mines, or the passage to the Pacific, whose existence they might have concealed for the benefit of a secret society to which they belonged. He then offered to repeat Verrazano's voyage and reveal these hidden findings. Francis I, who had already considered the matter, showed such enthusiasm that he told the navigator he would sponsor the voyage and pay all the expenses out of his own pocket.

Jacques Cartier's expedition set sail in January 1533 and arrived at the coast of Newfoundland after only three weeks. They encountered

King Francis I sponsored the voyage of Jacques Cartier in his competition with England. (Portrait of Francis I from around 1530, attributed to Jean Clouet.)

chunks of floating ice and saw great polar bears, whose size and snowy whiteness they described with amazement in their diary. A little farther on, something more surprising was awaiting them: a large fishing boat, whose captain told them he had come from La Rochelle to fish for cod and that his ship had drifted to the north. Cartier landed at an island he named Saint John, after the Essene Baptist revered by the Temple. His Templar message was more evident, when, upon reaching a small archipelago, he named it the Magdalen Islands, obviously in homage to Mary Magdalene, alleged wife of Jesus and mother of the Royal Blood, according to the Gnostics. It is curious, to say the least, that the mariner of Saint-Malo chose this name at a time when the cult of Mary Magdalene had been almost forgotten in France since the dissolution of the Temple by the Holy See.

In his contact with the natives, Cartier heard stories about the legendary Kingdom of Saguenay, the golden city of the Algonquins. According to his informers, this city was reached by going up the Saguenay River, a tributary of the Saint Lawrence. The navigator returned to France in 1534, ready to prepare a large expedition in search of that mythical city, where he hoped to find the true original settlement of the Templars of Henry Sinclair; since the region did not appear to have any gold mines, the Saguenay treasure could, in his opinion, have no origin other than the Temple.

In his second voyage, Jacques Cartier stayed longer in America and explored various islands in the Gulf of Saint Lawrence before going up the river of the same name. He reached the mouth of the Saguenay, wide and steep like a Norwegian fjord, then landed at Tadoussac, a kind of commercial port where the Huron Algonquins of the region exchanged merchandise with the Inuit of the north. But neither tribe knew anything about the Golden City. The expedition continued southwest along the Saint Lawrence, reaching the place where it suddenly narrows, at present-day Québec City. They continued upriver, arriving at a large town whose inhabitants called themselves the Hochelaga and showed the explorers their dwellings, which were arranged in a grid with a ceremonial square at the center. Cartier took possession of this place in the name of Francis I, and gave it the name Montréal (Royal Mountain), perhaps in allusion to Mount Zion and its mysterious Priory. In the modern-day city of Montréal, there is still a district called Hochelaga.

Cartier continued southwest and heard that certain tribes of Lake Superior made things from copper to trade with the Hurons for furs and other merchandise. But copper was not gold, and the French explorer decided to turn around and begin the return voyage. He did not find the Golden City of the Temple, but he opened the way for France to take possession of the vast Canadian territories that were to be disputed with the English over the next two centuries.

10

ARCADIA IN CANADA

The transatlantic expeditions of the sixteenth century, which mixed the desire for mythical treasures with the conquest and colonization of the New World, the slave trade, and the conversion of the native peoples, often took on an esoteric undertone. Not only the Templars themselves or their successors, the Knights of Christ and the Freemasons, went on voyages with missions or objectives relating to knowledge of a mysterious character. Other orders and secret societies also participated in various expeditions, openly or clandestinely, in pursuit of the fantastic enigmas offered by the continent rediscovered by Columbus.

The Navigators of the Order of Malta

It is known that in the eleventh century a group of Italian merchants from Amalfi founded a hospital in Jerusalem for pilgrims. At the end of that century, in 1099 (shortly before the founding of the Templars), the director of the hospital, a Provençal knight named Gerardo, founded a combatant order called the Military Order of Saint John of the Hospital, better known as the Hospitallers. Perhaps it was no coincidence that Gerardo chose the name of Saint John the Baptist—once again connecting the crusades with the Essene prophet—and that his principal fortified enclave was called Saint Jean d'Acre. One should remember that a branch of the Essenes, the Coptic Gnostics of Egypt, had spread its creed in the third and fourth centuries over all of the Levant, where members remained hidden beneath the Muslim domain.

When the Latin kingdom of Jerusalem succumbed to the attacks of Saladin in 1187, the Hospitallers withdrew to the fort of Saint Jean d'Acre and soon afterward sought refuge in Cyprus, from which they took possession of the Greek island of Rhodes. There they settled for over two centuries, during which time they participated in the political and religious intrigue of Europe, with the result that in 1312 Pope Clement V granted them a large part of the goods and privileges seized from the dissolved Order of the Temple. The two orders had been adversaries before, but from then on they became irreconcilable enemies. Charles V conquered Rhodes in 1530, but ceded the island of Malta, in the middle of the Mediterranean, to the Hospitallers. There they adopted the lengthy title of Sovereign Military Hospitaller Order of Saint John of Jerusalem, of Rhodes, and of Malta, which historians usually reduce to Sovereign Order of Malta. Their masters and knights fought bravely to maintain their island's independence for two more centuries, until Napoleon invaded it in 1798 and Great Britain dislodged the French two years later. The dismantled Order reorganized in Italy in the nineteenth century, and is still recognized as sovereign by several Western nations today, although without its own territory and with only charitable purposes.

Samuel de Champlain was born in La Rochelle in 1567. At that time, the historic port that had lodged the Phantom Fleet of the Templars was a cold and isolated city, in which—another coincidence—numerous Huguenot families lived in relative tranquillity. Samuel was Catholic, perhaps descended from converted Jews, but had dealings and friendships with many of his Protestant neighbors. All we know of him besides this is that he was an expert navigator, and that at a certain point in time he was contracted by Don Francisco Coloma, a Spanish mariner who was an admiral of the Royal Navy and not overly discreet about his membership in the Order of Malta. Another of the many coincidences that appear in this book is the surname of this knight—which, like that of Columbus, means "dove," and perhaps was also mysteriously changed from the original.

Admiral Coloma sent Champlain on his official voyages to America, during which the navigator from La Rochelle became familiar with transatlantic travel and the geography of the American coastlines. Once he had sufficient experience, his mentor recommended him to a member of the Sovereign Order, Vice Admiral Aymar de Clermont, who was lieutenant general of the colonies in America known as New France. Clermont put Champlain in contact with another Maltese knight, Isaac de Razilly, a ship's captain who proposed founding a priory in Nova Scotia from which the Order would govern New France. The two navigators outlined the plan of the expedition, but Razilly died shortly after arriving in the New World, and was buried at a site near Oak Island.

Upon his return to France, Samuel de Champlain went to Ardennes to visit a Huguenot named des Monts, bearing a letter of introduction written by Razilly shortly before his death. It is likely that in this interview, des Monts revealed his true identity: He was in reality Pietro del Monte, the Italian knight of Malta who had been Grand Master of the Order between 1568 and 1572. Upon retiring, he had moved to France and bought or leased a residence in the county of the family of Godfrey de Bouillon (another coincidence). Before this revelation, Champlain must have informed del Monte of the priory's project in Canada, thwarted by the death of their mutual friend Razilly.

In 1603, des Monts, or del Monte, asked for the king's authorization to establish a colonial company for fur trading in Canada. In this same year, he organized an expedition to Nova Scotia with three ships. The captain commanded his own ship, Champlain commanded another, and a member of the Order of Malta named Pont-Gravé commanded the third. After sailing together to Sable Island, they reached Mahone Bay, where Oak Island is located, but apparently Champlain either did not see it or confused it with another island, since he describes it in his diary as being covered with fir trees, with many oak trees growing on the nearby mainland. It is difficult to believe that the vegetation of the area could have changed so quickly since the visit of Henry Sinclair and the Templars. It is also surprising that Champlain named the archipelago the Islands of the Martyrs, considering that the so-called Canadian

Martyrs were a group of Jesuit missionaries from France massacred by the Iroquois in 1649, more than four decades after Samuel Champlain's voyage. It is possible that he chose this name in homage to James Gunn, Sinclair's lieutenant who had been killed along with a few companions two centuries before. But why would a knight of Malta make such a gesture to the Templars? Perhaps it was because at the time his true enemies were the members of the Company of Jesus, the new order created by the Holy See to spread its creed and further its worldly interests, among other missions.

The Jesuits were (and are) enlightened men, enamored of knowledge and aware of the realities of the world, but very rigid and severe in the execution of their mission. Their first battle, against the permissive order of Saint-Sulpice, began in Europe and rapidly moved to America, where ships and colonists swarmed from various European kingdoms.

Numerous ships from Basque country and French ports such as Saint-Malo and La Rochelle practiced the clandestine poaching of whales. Their center of activity and dispute was the region between Québec, which Champlain had founded as a port and fur-trading post in 1608, and the anchorage of Tadoussac. On this last point, Pont-Gravé insisted on reproaching the whalers who infringed on French fishing laws, and when he intervened in the dispute, the colonial authorities confiscated the three ships of his expedition.

Soon numerous Catholic families had settled in Québec; those persecuted by the bloody religious wars in Europe fled there immediately. The French admiralty had granted the Caen brothers, Protestant explorers of Jewish origin, a license to found colonies in Canada. Soon Québec was full of Huguenots, who eventually outnumbered the Catholic population. The Sulpicians tried to maintain coexistence, but the Jesuits succeeded in getting the king to revoke the license of the Caen brothers and forced the Huguenots to march to the south. Champlain and his fellow members had to abandon the idea of starting a priory of the Order of Malta, and the open war between the two religious orders destroyed the possibility of forming a united New France under the prudent governance of the Crown.

The Knights of
the Most Holy Sacrament

In 1630, Henry de Levis, duke of Ventadour, completed the formation of a new order that had been organized three years earlier: the Company of the Most Holy Sacrament of the Altar. Although the designation "company" bore Jesuit connotations, it is probable that the founder adopted it not in homage to the followers of Saint Ignatius of Loyola, but rather as a challenge. Levis had a history and connections with the whole range of secret societies and Hermetic Christology. One of his ancestors, Isabel de Levis, was the mother of Marie de Saint Clair, successor of the first historic Grand Master of the Priory of Sion, and Henry himself claimed to be descended from the lineage of Mary, mother of Jesus. The name Levis was indisputably of Jewish origin, coming from the tribe of Levi, the third son of Jacob. The Levites had been Hebrew priests since biblical times, dedicated exclusively to worship and the city of the temple. Levis and Levi were common patronymics in Jewish communities and the southern France of the Cathars and Huguenots.

Just like the Templars, the Knights of the Most Holy Sacrament initially numbered nine, most of them being of noble birth. The following names are mentioned: Maria de Medici, former queen of France, exiled from Paris after her disagreement with Richelieu; Henri de Pichery, a noble of the royal family who was an ambassador in Rome; Father Suffren, confessor of King Louis XIII; the archbishop of Arles; the marquis of Andelot; and the influential Capuchin monk Philippe d'Angoumois. Levis was the nephew of the second duke of Montmorency, who had defeated a fleet of Huguenots near the Canadian island of Oleron in 1625. The king had made him grand admiral of New France and ceded extensive colonial territories to him. Henri de Levis planned to buy some of these territories from his uncle in order to achieve his company's objectives.

The statutes of the company established that its mission was to assist the needy, just like so many other associations of aristocrats who hoped to compensate for their enormous privilege by doing deeds of charity for the poor. However, Henri de Levis and his companions behaved as if they were in a secret society. Only they knew who the other members of the company were, and they met at a different place each time. Their papers and documents never bore names or signatures, and they were identified only with the seal that represented the Most Holy Sacrament. Although some of their activities really did involve aiding the destitute, they were not allowed to boast of this publicly, or to share these labors with ecclesiastic authorities, despite the fact that there were always prelates and clergy among their members. In the following years, a number of very notable and quite diverse individuals joined the company. Among them was Nicolas Pavillon, the Jansenist bishop of the little-known diocese of Alet in the Cathar province of Languedoc, where works and activities took place similar to those later undertaken by the priest Saunière at the mysterious Rennes-le-Château.

Another well-known sacramentist was Vicente de Paul, canonized by the Church despite his suspicious ancestors. Ordained a priest in Toulouse, one of the ancient centers of Catharism, he spent three years in Tunis, supposedly as a prisoner of the Berber pirates. There he was a disciple of an Egyptian alchemist who instructed him in the occult sciences, and upon his return to Europe, he went to Avignon to display his arts of black magic before the papal delegation. The pontifical dignitary, rather than being indignant, entrusted Vicente with a secret mission in Paris connected with the king's inner circle. Soon Vicente acquired an impressive fortune, which he devoted to works of charity directed to prisoners condemned to the galleys, inmates in dungeons, and other people in need. At the same time, he was admitted into the circles of high society, in which he played the part of a rich and pious benefactor. When the Germans occupied Lorraine in the Thirty Years War, many nobles of that region who had aided him in becoming rich sought refuge in Paris. The grateful cleric then diverted almost all the funds of his works of charity toward the dispossessed aristocrats and their noble families. Soon afterward, Vicente de Paul founded the Congregation of Saint Lazarus, known for its veneration of the Black Virgin, and later joined the Company of the Most Holy Sacrament in time to transmit his hermetic knowledge to them.

Undoubtedly, for its mission of installing a priory in New France, the most significant member of the company was Jean-Jacques Olier. A young Parisian from a good family, he had been led into religion by Francisco de Sales, who frequented the house of his parents. He was

ordained a priest when he joined the Company of the Most Holy Sacrament at the hands of his teacher Vicente de Paul. The young cleric
varied his mysterious calling with fervent participation in the works of
charity sponsored by Vicente. Such dedication did not prevent him from
mingling in high society, thanks partly to the fortune he had inherited
from his father. In August 1641, the curate of Saint-Sulpice, in the tur-
bulent district of Saint-Germain, offered to sell his position to Olier.
In this parish, the secret knight of the Most Holy Sacrament founded
the Saint-Sulpice Seminary, where he preached the renewal of Catholicism with surreptitious allusions to the Christianity of the time before
Constantine, and even to Saint Paul, spreading the ideology of the Essenes and Gnostics. The Sulpicians did not formally constitute a religious
order, but their seminaries spread rapidly throughout France and its
colonies in America, where they preached tolerance for the Huguenots.
We have already mentioned their confrontations with the Jesuits of New
France for this reason, after the establishment of numerous missions and
churches on both sides of the Saint Lawrence River.

The most emblematic temple built by the Sulpicians in Canada is the
great church of Notre Dame de Montréal. It is not known whether it
was constructed by Jean-Jacques Olier himself on a clandestine visit not
recorded in his biography or (more likely) by the mysterious Sulpician
Paul de Chomedey, lord of Maisonneuve, his delegate in New France.
What is certain is that the society formed around Notre Dame governed
the city in practice, and that the majority of its members were Knights
of the Most Holy Sacrament. Meanwhile, Olier, seeing the necessity of
educating poor children, founded a special branch of the order with this
purpose. Shortly afterward, this branch became an autonomous order
under the direction of the priest La Salle, a reformist pedagogue whose
Christian name, by clear predestination, was Jean-Baptiste.

Mary Magdalene and the Black Virgin

Some Canadian experts in Christology claim that the Sulpicians built
Notre Dame de Montréal as an obvious homage to the Virgin Mary,
but that the Knights of the Most Holy Sacrament secretly dedicated this
temple to Mary Magdalene. The Gnostic Evangelists and the traditions

of the Temple suggested that she was the wife of Jesus, with whom he produced descendants. Thus, while the Virgin represented the pure white face of the ancestral Mother Goddess, Mary Magdalene embodied her dark side, more human, sinful, and sensual. It is said that the Templars saluted each other by calling themselves Sons of the Widow, and it is certain that according to these sources, Magdalene was the first follower of Christ to reach France.

In certain places all over Europe, images of a Virgin with dark skin are venerated, a worship that also exists in America. The congregation of Saint Lazarus, founded by Vicente de Paul, dedicated the church of Notre Dame de Marseilles in the Languedoc to the cult of the Black Virgin. The Lazarists were habitual guests of the curate Saunière in his estate of Rennes-le-Château, where they participated in strange rites and ceremonies.

1 1

PIRATES AND FREEMASONS IN AMERICAN INDEPENDENCE

Freemasonry, or the Order of the Temple under its veil, had a fundamental influence on the process of American independence, as much in the English and French colonies as in the Spanish ones. The majority of the ideologists and leaders of the colonies' rebellions were Freemasons, who turned the local elite against the imperial powers. Naval combat had great importance in these revolutionary wars, the lead parts being played by pirates and privateers of a Masonic persuasion.

A Free Land for the "New Jerusalem"

The secret objectives of Freemasonry differed with respect to the liberation of the British and Spanish colonies. Since the times of Henry Sinclair, or maybe before, the Templars had aspired to establish their "New Jerusalem" in North America, whose natural riches and geographical advantages they knew well. Those legendary coasts of "Vinland" and "Estotiland" were completely colonized and densely populated at the end of the eighteenth century by descendants of English corsairs and French buccaneers, among others. The Templar ideals of those navigators and colonists had remained alive, and numerous more or less secret lodges existed, linked to European Freemasonry.

In the case of the Spanish viceroyalty, captains, and governors in America, the objectives of Freemasonry were more political and strategic. The aims were to weaken the Spanish empire and, if possible, to destroy it, completing the work of the Templar pirates and corsairs of the previous centuries. At the same time, the Temple had an old score to settle with the Vatican and the kingdom most faithful to it. This plan was based upon the liberal rebellions that were brewing in France and in Spain itself, erupting with varying success before the end of the century.

According to the Temple's millenary project, the emancipated colonies should form two great federations of united states, one in the north and the other in the south. Both would maintain brotherly equilibrium and help each other to prosper and strengthen, aiding each other against foreign attacks or interferences. In this way, the whole New World would become the ancestral Arcadia or lost Atlantis, revived by imposing a new order upon the world.

Freemasonry and the Thirteen Colonies

By the mid-eighteenth century, the English had established thirteen colonies along the Atlantic coast of North America, reaching from New Hampshire to Georgia. At the same time, France and Spain were disputing the adjacent territories, reacting to the aggressive politics of imperial expansion encouraged by Prime Minister William Pitt. Some of the cities in these first thirteen colonies, such as Philadelphia, New York, Boston, and Charleston, prospered throughout the eighteenth century, during which their population multiplied through the arrival of immigrants, principally European. The colonial ports maintained considerable commerce with the homeland, but this began to be affected by the high taxes imposed in 1765 upon the monopolistic trade of British products. The colonies rose up in protest, forcing London to abolish the new taxes, except for those on tea.

In 1773, at a tavern in Boston called the Green Dragon, the members of the Masonic lodge of Saint Andrew met to exchange news from the other colonies and discuss the situation. On the demand of Grand Master John Hancock—one of the signatories of the Declaration of

Independence—they decided to take revolutionary action, and a few days afterward they appeared at Boston Harbor dressed as Mohawk Indians. There they made revolutionary proclamations and expressed their protest by seizing the boxes of tea that were being unloaded from an English ship and throwing them into the water. The theatrical model spread, and a year later in Philadelphia, the first Continental Congress took place, a meeting of colonial leaders who urged the people to resist and boycott British products. This action had great repercussions, thanks to the activity of the old pirates, who had become smugglers of the most indispensable merchandise. England responded by suspending the autonomy of Massachusetts, the main seat of the rebels, and closing the port of Boston for breaking the laws that prohibited contraband. The colonies then began organizing armed militias to fight the imperial oppression.

We will not relate the ups and downs of the war of the English colo-

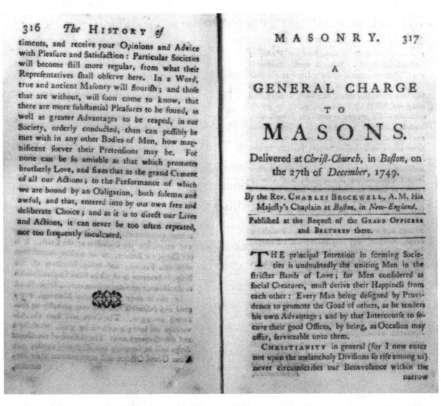

Boston was one of the first centers where Freemasonry was established in the American colonies.

Masonic apron presented to General Washington by Lafayette's wife. (Robert Macoy, General History, Cyclopedia and Dictionary of Freemasonry, *1850.)*

nies against the homeland; suffice it to say that it resulted in the Declaration of Independence of the United States of America in 1776. On July 4 of that year, the representatives of the thirteen rebel colonies signed the founding act. Nine of these delegates were known and committed Freemasons, among them the three who had drawn up the text—Benjamin Franklin, Thomas Jefferson, and John Adams—as well as their intellectual inspiration, Thomas Paine.

When General George Washington took his oath of office as the first president of the United States of America, he wore a Masonic apron during the ceremony. According to tradition, it was embroidered by the wife of Lafayette, the French revolutionary aristocrat who had fought

George Washington decorated with the Masonic apron. (Anonymous portrait.)

alongside Washington. No fewer than fifteen other generals of the revolutionary army belonged to Masonic orders, an ideology that was equally prevalent among the lower-ranking officers. In fact, it is difficult to find a more widespread ideological or religious affiliation in the emancipation, constitution, and consolidation of the United States. The majority of the country's founders were Freemasons, and Masonic ideology and symbolism are present in many elements of the identity of this powerful nation, everywhere from its fundamental institutions to the dollar bill and the Statue of Liberty. It is another question whether these ideologies really led to the founding of the New Arcadia dreamed of by the founders.

The Privateers and the Revolution

As previous chapters of this book have shown, the Order of the Temple had a decisive presence in the history of navigation. After the Order's foundation in the twelfth century, Templar mariners sailed the seas of the world as merchant captains, pirates, explorers, corsairs, discoverers, or colonists. This tradition, like others that characterized the Temple, doubtless passed into Freemasonry, which maintained this ideology among men of the sea. It is not strange, then, that the Freemasons who led the rebellion of the thirteen English colonies turned to their sailing brothers to fight against imperial oppression.

In the autumn of 1775, the British fleet easily blocked the "illegal" commerce of the rebellious colonies, and harassed their ports and coastal populations. In response, some of the Masonic governors of the rebel provinces met with their seafaring brothers to charter privateer ships to defend their waters. However, the majority of the Continental Congress did not want to aggravate hostilities, some even trusting in the possibility of making a treaty with the homeland. When it became evident that England had no intention of negotiating anything, the possession of a rebel fleet became an urgent priority. This was the only way to defend the ports, protect the trading of vital goods, fight British ships, and acquire from other nations the arms and resources necessary for the resistance.

The first action of the incipient Continental Navy, dependent on Congress, was to equip two ships, each with ten cannons and a crew of eighty men recruited from among civilian sailors and commanded by an army officer or merchant captain without experience in naval combat. Their first mission was a three-month voyage to intercept the transport ships carrying supplies and munitions for the British troops. The operation was not a great success, and despite becoming more unified later, the fleet of the Continental Congress met only with failure in its battles with the Royal Navy. After the disasters of the Delaware River in 1777, Maine in 1779, and Charleston in 1780, it was practically dismantled and had no operative capacity.

The naval front was then turned over to the squadrons of the states, and particularly to the privateers, chartered and commanded by Freemasons, who also took the reins of the Continental Navy and used it to transport funds and arms provided by the European lodges and establish relations with the French revolutionaries. In reality, several squadrons of privateers had continued to act alongside Congress's fleet, such as the one maintained by the Masonic government of Pennsylvania, or "Washington's Navy," created by the generals of the revolutionary army.

The majority of scholars who write about the naval history of the United States recognize that the naval front of the Revolution was in the hands of the privateers, although they tend not to admit that most of them were Freemasons. Their ships comprised everything from warships, heavily armed for combat, to merchant vessels with artillery, authorized to capture other enemy merchants. These ships or fleets were largely independent of the central and state governments but subject to some regulations, such as licenses known as "letters of reprisal" that authorized them to take spoils on the condition that the owners of the vessels deposit guarantees in coin for the conduct of their privateers.

When a privateer captured a ship, he was not allowed to destroy it, sack it, or take possession of it, but had to bring it to the American port from which he had sailed. If this condition was fulfilled (which did not always happen), a tribunal called a Court of the Admiralty decided whether or not the capture had been appropriate. If the capture was considered legitimate, the ship and its cargo would be put up for auction and sold. The resulting money would be divided between the sponsor and the privateer and his crew, according to a contract drawn up prior to undertaking the voyage. This doubtless had an influence on the decline of the Navy of the Congress, considering that a reasonably successful privateer could earn ten times the salary of a naval captain.

It is calculated that during the War of Independence and the post-revolutionary period, the United States armed between two and three thousand private pirate ships, which preyed upon British maritime commerce until this practice was declared illegal at the Convention of Paris in 1856. An American historian wrote: "Valuable service to the country was rendered by the privateers, and they contributed in a large degree to the naval defense, and so to the fortunate outcome of the war. On the other hand, the system was subject to abuses and was in many ways detrimental to the regular naval service." A contemporary wrote that the American pirates damaged Britain in its "pride far more than its pocketbook," putting the prestige of the Royal Navy in jeopardy.

The Liberators and the Masonic Lodges

It is not possible to analyze the process of independence of the Spanish colonies in America without taking into account two events in Europe that were also led by Masonic lodges. The first, and more important for the world's history, was the French Revolution of 1789, which occurred soon after the independence of the United States and was born of the same ideology of liberty. The second, in some way linked to the first, was the series of liberal rebellions in Spain that led to the Cortes at Cadiz and the constitution of 1812.

The French revolutionary movement began with the storming of the Bastille. It cost the king and queen their heads, and produced both the Terror and the Declaration of the Rights of Man, the model mirrored by all the major figures of the Latin American revolutions. The intellectual inspiration and ideological background of the French Revolution was the Enlightenment: a rationalist, liberal, and secular movement that furthered scientific knowledge and implacably questioned dogmatic religious obscurantism. Many of the major thinkers of the Age of Enlightenment, if not all, were linked to Freemasonry—such as Montesquieu, Voltaire, Rousseau, and probably Diderot.

Lafayette: Hero of Two Revolutions

Gilbert du Montier, Marquis de Lafayette, was born in 1757 into a French military and naval family initiated to Freemasonry. He attained the rank of cavalry captain at age sixteen and went on to a brilliant career in the army. Four years later, at the suggestion of his lodge, he bought a ship and sailed for America together with other French Freemasons to fight the English. There he heroically led several battles, which earned him the rank of major general and a place on the staff of Grand Master George Washington. After the victory at Yorktown, Lafayette returned to Paris to collaborate with the American ambassadors (and Freemasons) Benjamin Franklin and Thomas Jefferson.

His position in the following years was more controversial, perhaps because of dissent and contradictions within Freemasonry itself. He tried to defend the constitutional monarchy, and as commander of the National Guard harshly repressed popular revolts, losing almost all his

The vacillations of Pope Pius VI regarding the French Revolution continued on the occasion of Napoleon's entrance into Italy, speeding the erosion of pontifical power. (Jacques-Louis David: Equestrian Portrait of Napoleon, Wilbert *Collection, Paris.)*

popularity. He returned to lead the revolution that overthrew the Bourbons in 1830, but turned down the offer of being president of a new republic, and instead had Louis-Philippe crowned as a constitutional monarch. Shortly before dying in 1834, he went back to advocating the reinstallation of a democratic republic.

Masons and Revolutionaries in South America

It is said that it was General Lafayette who, during the American War of Independence, nominated Lieutenant Colonel Francisco de Miranda to become a Freemason. They may have met after the Battle of Pensacola in 1781. Both were foreign volunteers and excellent combatants, and without doubt coincided in their libertarian ideals. In spite of their high military ranks, the Frenchman was barely twenty-four years old and the Venezuelan not yet thirty. Their lives as revolutionaries had only just begun.

Miranda, born in Caracas in 1750, abandoned his studies of philosophy to launch into an adventurous and idealistic life. After participating in the Revolution of the Three Provinces and becoming a Freemason, he was a smuggler in Havana, working against the Spanish monopoly. Accused by the Inquisition of owning prohibited books, he was deported to Oran, in Algeria, in 1783. He fled from there with the aid of American agents and began a long trip through the Masonic lodges of Europe, seeking aid for his projects of independence. Finally, in Paris in 1797, he brought together the main revolutionary leaders of the Spanish colonies, including his compatriot Andrés Bello, the Chilean Bernardo O'Higgins, the Ecuadoran Vicente Rocafuerte, and his young colleague from Guayaquil, José Joaquín Olmedo, among many others. They all committed themselves to aid the revolutionary movement through their respective lodges, which were coordinated by the "American Lodge" formed a few years earlier in London.

In 1811, the Lodge of London summoned the Spanish colonel José de San Martín, from Rio de la Plata, who had fought heroically three years earlier at the Battle of Bailén. The young military man received the order to return to South America to strengthen the uprising that had begun in Buenos Aires the previous year. This movement was inspired by the economist and intellectual (and Freemason) Mariano Moreno, who led the most radical wing of the independence movement. Moreno died mysteriously at sea the following year, during a voyage to participate in a meeting of the Lodge of London. Perhaps this spurred San Martín's intention to form an army, cross the Andes, and meet with O'Higgins, who was commanding the rebel troops at the military headquarters of Chile. The plan was coordinated by the Lodge of Lautaro, formed expressly for this purpose.

San Martín arrived in Buenos Aires in 1812 and placed himself in the service of the provisional government. His first action was to form a regular regiment of grenadiers, with which he drove back the Spaniards who were marauding along the banks of the Rio de la Plata, fighting with the aid of Hipólito Bouchard, the Masonic privateer of French origin. Afterward he took charge of the so-called Army of the North, with which he carried out a successful campaign that permitted him to unite the revolutionary territory and bring his army across the steep range of the Andes. Bernardo O'Higgins, who had been defeated by the Spanish at Rancagua, came to unite with San Martín, and the two launched a victorious reconquest of Chile, which installed O'Higgins as supreme governor.

Meanwhile, Miranda, taking advantage of the resistance to Joseph Bonaparte in Spain and the convocation of the Cortes at Cadiz, had obtained the aid of the English and American lodges for two revolutionary expeditions to Venezuela, which were defeated. But his ideas had planted a fertile seed, and in 1811 a rebellion for independence broke out, led by the young colonel (and Freemason) Simon Bolívar, with whom Miranda hastened to unite. The Masonic strategy for liberating the South American colonies now consisted of the simultaneous advance of both military revolutionary leaders, San Martín from the south and Bolívar from the north, enclosing the Spanish armies in a "pincer" that left them no possible escape. To aid this plan, many Masonic privateers guarded the Pacific coast to stop reinforcements coming by sea from Central America and Mexico.

San Martín put his army and supplies aboard a squadron of these privateers and sailed from the port of Valparaíso in September 1820.

His intent was to attack the viceroyalty of Peru, where Antonio José de Sucre, the military Freemason of Catalan origin, had risen up in arms. The two managed to defeat the Spanish and entered Lima in August of the following year. San Martín declared the independence of Peru, as he had done with Chile. The victorious general had now liberated three new nations: the United Provinces of Rio de la Plata (now Argentina and Uruguay) and the republics of Chile and Peru.

Meanwhile, Bolívar had confronted numerous political and military difficulties, among them Miranda's resignation and the Spanish reconquest of Caracas. But he rebuilt his forces with the aid of Henri Christophe, the Black "King" of Haiti, and returned to fight until achieving the liberation of Venezuela and his designation as supreme leader of the republic. In 1818, in compliance with the plan established by Freemasonry, he started the so-called Campaign of the Center, the purpose of which was to liberate present-day Colombia and Ecuador by closing the "pincers" and meeting with San Martín. In August of the following year he entered Bogotá, liberated Quito together with Sucre, and united all these territories with Venezuela to form Gran Colombia. This vast land was named in homage to the great navigator (and Freemason) who had made official the existence of the New World that unjustly bore another explorer's name.

Finally, in July 1822, the two triumphant liberators met in the Ecuadoran city of Guayaquil. There they held their famous secret interview, the contents of which have yet to be obtained by historians, sparking polemical debates even today. What is known is that as a result of this meeting, San Martín renounced all his claims and titles, leaving the remainder of the campaign and the corresponding honors to Bolívar. The Liberator of the South soon accepted the offer of a French lodge to occupy a residence in Boulogne-sur-Mer, on the English Channel, where he spent the rest of his life until dying at a very advanced age in 1850. What led the hero of three nations to abandon everything just when he was reaching the height of his career? What did he and Bolívar talk about in Guayaquil that led him to make this irrevocable decision? Official Argentine history suggests a "heroic renunciation" due to lack of support from the governor of Buenos Aires. Some revisionist historians claim that San Martín suffered a grave secret ailment, which is unlikely considering his longevity; or that his austere character was frustrated with the ambitious conceit of Simon Bolívar, which seems more credible given the known extreme temperament of the Venezuelan liberator. But it is not very likely that San Martín, if he disliked Bolívar's personality, would have given him his army and conquests in addition to the glorious merit of having achieved South American independence.

From the Masonic point of view, the interpretation is much simpler. San Martín, misled by his Messianic beliefs or by local political commitments, had committed a grave error with respect to the plan of the American Lodge of London. In establishing three independent nations in the south of the continent, he contradicted and blocked Bolívar's campaign to create Gran Colombia, uniting all the liberated Spanish colonies. The Freemasons decided to get the Argentine out of the way and put the Venezuelan at the head of operations. It was this that Bolívar communicated to San Martín in the famous meeting, and the latter's "heroic renunciation" consisted of complying with this mandate with a dignified resignation.

In 1830, despite Bolívar's efforts, Venezuela seceded from Gran Colombia, beginning the disintegration of what his dreams had realized. The liberator, resentful and sick, resigned from his position and took refuge at a friend's plantation, where he died in the same year. The Masonic project was not completed, despite the military and political success of the plan to liberate the South American colonies. The true power behind the governors of the new republics ended up being their eternal rival, the Catholic Church, which from the beginning had sent "revolutionary" clerics to infiltrate the meetings and activities of the rebels. The Vatican later deployed all its forces in the various political and social strata, also taking advantage of the strong Catholicism implanted by the missionaries since the times of the Conquistadors that pervaded all classes of people. It was then sufficient for the Church and its agents to encourage the nationalist and patriotic sentiments that characterized the young nations, creating a xenophobia that manifested especially against neighboring nations. Latin America spent all of the nineteenth century, and part of the twentieth, embroiled in conflicts over borders and fratricidal wars, definitively preventing a continental union.

The Mysterious Retreat of Freemasonry

The United States, which at first had almost openly aided the forces of Latin American independence, completely changed the course of its politics toward the region at the beginning of the twentieth century. To try to understand this abandonment of the great Masonic project for the Americas, it is fitting to return briefly to the internal events of North America. The original thirteen colonies expanded during the nineteenth century to a large territory reaching from the Canadian border to the north to the Rio Grande to the south, where many new states were established, bought, or taken by force from France, Spain, and Mexico. The majority Latin and Catholic population of these territories was augmented by African slaves and immigrants from Europe and elsewhere, which diversified its ethnic and religious makeup. The Freemasons saw their influence diluted, and they entrenched themselves in the northern states. There they encouraged industrial development and the ideas of modernization that formed part of their project, while the rest of the country maintained its primitive rural composition in the small farms of the Midwest, the rich slave plantations of the South, and the cattle ranches that flourished in the pioneering of the West.

Freemasonry versus Slavery

The resistance of the southern states to restriction or abolition of the fruitful (from their perspective) slave system provoked continuous friction with the northern states, dominated by Masonic governors. Slavery contradicted the moral ideology of Freemasonry and obstructed its project of imposing an egalitarian democracy based on modernity and industrialization. This continued into the presidency of Abraham Lincoln, a brilliant antislavery lawyer and conspicuous member of the Lodge of Illinois. The mere accession of Lincoln to office provoked rebellion among the southerners, who formed a confederacy independent of the Union. The episodes of the Civil War between the North and South are well known (and extensively documented by literature and film), and its outcome was favorable for the Union. A few days after his victory, Lincoln was assassinated by (according to one theory) a mercenary employed by the Vatican.

Perhaps it was no great solution to convert the black slaves of the southern plantations into proletarian workers in the factories of the North, but Abraham Lincoln went down in history as the great leader of American liberalism, and with him Freemasonry fought its last battle for power.

The presidency of the conservative populist Theodore Roosevelt marked a radical change in the foreign policy of the United States, advocating an aggressive expansionism into Latin America and creating an "American Zone" in 1904 to construct and administer the Panama Canal. From then on, the United States treated Central America as its property, constantly resorting to political pressure or acts of sabotage to remove politicians and put replacements in power who served its purposes, including various criminal dictators. The main objective of American "big stick politics," apart from the obvious economic exploitation and strategic positioning, was to prevent these subjugated countries from uniting to liberate themselves once more from oppression. It became clear that the prophetic phrase of James Monroe, claiming "America for the Americans," actually meant "Latin America for the North Americans."

It is not easy to explain why Freemasonry lost control of this great land of North America that had cost it so much to liberate—taking into account above all that it had come to dominate all resources of power, and that the Catholic Church did not have many forces to resist Freemasonry there. Some scholars have explained it as the result of a sudden rupture of Freemasonry's tacit alliances with the Protestant creeds, or of internal dissent among the various lodges. Another reason, more worthy of consideration, claims that the Freemasons' own ideology of democracy, modernization, and political transparency overcame their antiquated practices of secrecy and their ancient pyramidal organization. It is possible that both factors acted in synergy to displace Freemasonry, or that the Freemasons decided to continue acting in secrecy in order not to contaminate themselves with circumstantial interests or compromises. It must not be forgotten that the mission of the Temple is in essence millenary, both in the sense that it originated many thousands of years ago and in the sense that one day, before the end of time, it will prevail.

CONCLUSION

I believe that in this book I have offered sufficient data to demonstrate a thrilling, mysterious history that lies parallel to and beneath official history. The Order of the Temple and other secret societies, such as the pirates and other navigators, were the main characters in this underground current of ideas and events that has been hidden by powerful leaders, the Church, and their scribes.

The main thread of this secret history leads back to wisdom that is ancestral, perhaps even antediluvian, transmitting an inalienable legacy to a few initiates: that of preserving the memory of the absolute force that rules the Universe, and using all possible resources, including the esoteric arts that form part of this legacy, to build a new society—in other words, to instill in humanity the cosmic values of harmony, peace, and spirituality, which permits people to live in the highest dimension of existence.

One or many successive Hermetic societies carefully preserved this legacy over the millennia, and tried to move forward in the accomplishment of their mission. In historical times, Egyptian priests, biblical prophets, Hebrew kabbalists, Essenes, early Christians, and Gnostics were some of the guardians and executors of the millenary message. According to esoteric Christology, Jesus of Nazareth was the greatest of them all, a true "Chosen One," founder of a lineage destined to endure as a reference and guarantee of the redemption of humankind.

The symbol of this continuity was the Holy Grail, the chalice that held the blood of Christ at the Last Supper and was later saved by St. Lawrence, corresponding phonetically to the *Sang Real* carried forward by the descendants of the Redeemer and Mary Magdalene. These symbols, together with the knowledge and secrets of ancestral wisdom and the proofs of the relationship between the sacred lineage and the Merovingian kings, form what initiates call the Great Secret.

In the Middle Ages, the Great Secret was entrusted to the Priory of Sion, whose Grand Master Bernard de Clairvaux created the Cistercian Order and soon afterward promoted the foundation of the Order of the Temple. In both cases, his intent was to destroy the severe mystic Hermeticism of the Priory and intervene directly in the spiritual and temporal matters of the world in competition with the Vatican, principal repressor and adulterator of the truths revealed by the Great Secret. In a word, he intended for the Cistercians to promote a covert rebellion against the Holy See, while the Temple openly gained political and economic power to fight the pope on his own ground.

As is known, with the Renaissance the struggle for true power shifted from land wars to the conquest of the sea. The great European kingdoms began to discover, conquer, and exploit the unknown lands beyond the oceans, and the Templars became pirate navigators, or used other pirates, to harass the ships that transported plundered riches from those lands.

The rest of this fascinating occult history is told in the preceding pages, in a story whose fundamental aspects can be summarized thus:

- Since the times of Greece and Rome, and even before, pirates were an archetype of free living and adventure, detached from any authority or law established by governments of their time.
- At the same time, they had their own code of conduct—egalitarian, tolerant, generous, and respectful of individual decisions. These rules coincided in part with the rules of the Temple, and both codes influenced each other without conflict.
- The Templars dedicated themselves to piracy, fleeing from cruel persecution by the pope, the king of France, and later the Inquisition. Thus, an inevitable desire for vengeance was added to their secret mission of destroying the Holy See.

- Numerous knights of the Temple managed to escape in their fleet when it sailed secretly from La Rochelle, and a group of them took refuge in the lands ruled by Henry Sinclair in the Orkneys and the north of Scotland.

- Influenced by stories of Viking voyages across the Atlantic, Sinclair sailed on an expedition for the purpose of hiding the Great Secret in these unknown lands. He buried this treasure, possibly on Oak Island, and remains of Templar settlements have been discovered in certain places in the United States.

- The majority of the great corsairs of the golden age of piracy were Templars, or had some relationship to the Order. In a subsidiary manner, their fabulous spoils and their precious maps and observations laid the foundations for colonist imperialism, especially that of Britain.

- Whatever the misty origins of Freemasonry might be, this society existed publicly between the sixteenth and eighteenth centuries in Scotland, England, and France. It is highly probable that the Masons were infiltrated by the Templars and became a cover for their purposes and activities.

- Columbus had a close link to the Templars, if he was not indeed a member of the Order. His mysterious origin and history suggest that he hid his true identity, and he used nautical and cartographic data that was in the possession only of the Temple for his "voyage to the Indies."

- The Templars, through Freemasonry, had a decisive influence and played an important role in the revolutions for independence in the Americas in the eighteenth and nineteenth centuries. In this process of liberation, they frequently acted as pirates in aid of the revolutionaries, and occasionally fought in naval battles.

It remains only to point out a phenomenon of the present day: the great interest that has arisen in the last few years in everything connected with secret societies and the truth about them, reflected in numerous studies, explorations, academic publications, and best sellers. Perhaps this is no coincidence, and the Grand Masters have decided that the time has come to reveal some of their secrets, believing that exposing their history to public opinion could be a way to destroy the barriers to knowing the truth imposed by the dominant powers and, we shall say again, by the secret designs of the Vatican. Perhaps thus the day will come on which the Holy See governs a merciful and humanist religion.

On that day, the Templars and other secret societies will occupy their place in history, with no more or less relevance than the other people and events that have carved out the destiny of the human race.

INDEX

Adams, John, 163
Aegean Sea, 9–12
Aethelstan, King, 99, 101
Ailly, Pierre d', 133
Alexander VI, Pope, 52
Alfonso IV, King, 41–42
Alfonso of Aragon, 37, 39
Algiers, 48–49
Alonso, Martín, 47–48
American Revolution, 165–67
Ango, Jean d', 145–46
Antonius, Marcus, 15–16
Apprentice Pillar, 103, *104*
Arcadia, 97, 137, 140, 141–43, 146–48,
    152–59. *See also* New World
architecture, 35–36, *35–37*, 94, 128–29
Aristotle, 99, 133
Ashmole, Elias, 104
Augustus, Philip, 33
Azores, 52

Bacon, Francis, 82–83, 104–5, 123–24
Bacon, Nicholas, 82
Baldwin II, 27–28
Berbers, 12, 48–49
Bernard, Saint, 29–31
Blackbeard, 70–72, *72*
Black Death, 47
Black Virgin, 157, 158–59
Blondel, Robert, 57
Bois, Jambe de, 52
Bolívar, Simon, 170

Bonny, Anne, 76, 77, 78–79, 89
Bonny, James, 76
Bontemps, Jean de, 57
Book of Enoch, 97, 99
Bouillon, Godfrey de, 26, 28
Brendan the Navigator, Saint, 113–14
Brotherhood of the Coast, 58, 65–66
buccaneers, 6, 54–57

Caesar, Julius, 15, *15*
Calico Jack, 75–80
Canada, 152–59
Canary Islands, 52, 112
Cartagena, 59
Carthaginians, 112–13
Cartier, Jacques, 59
Casenove, Guillaume de, 131
Cathars, 57, 80, *80*
cathedrals, 93–97, *94*
Catholics and Catholicism, 25, 105–6,
    140, 155
Cecil, William, 61
Champagne, Hugo de, 29, 30
Champlain, Samuel de, 153–54
Charlemagne, 81
Charles II, King, 105
Charles V, King of Spain, 54, 55, 57
Chartres cathedral, 36–37, *37*
Christophe, Henri, 171
Clairvaux, Bernard de, 29–31, 32, 35,
    176
Clement III, Pope, 33

Clement V, Pope, 39
Clement XII, Pope, 105
Clermont, Aymar de, 154
codfish, 114
Coligny, Gaspar de, 59
Coloma, Francisco, 153–54
Columbus, Christopher, 24, 42, 48,
    108–9
  crown jewels and, 138–39
  Judaism and, 138–39
  marriage of, 131–34
  mystery of, 125–28, *127*
  setbacks of, 134–36
  Templars and, 139–40
Company of the Most Holy Sacrament
    of the Altar, 156–58
Cook, James, 90
Coote, Richard, 67, 70
corsairs, 7, 60–80, 73–75, 84–86
Counter-Reformation, 58
Cousin, Jean, 113, 144
Crassus, 15
crown jewels, 123, 138–39
Crusades, 25–27, 33
Culliford, Robert, 69
Cuthbert, Saint, 18

Dampier, William, 88
Dead Sea Scrolls, 97, 99
Dieppe, Normandy, 143–46
Diodorus, 112, 113
Drake, Francis, 6, 61–65, *64*, 82–83
druids, 36, *36*
Drummond, John, 132

East India Company, 69–70
Edessa, 26, 33
Elizabeth I, 60, *60*, 61, 62, 63–64
Enlightenment, 167
Enriquez, King Alfonso, 128
Erik the Red, 17–18, 109, 116
Esquemeling, John, 88
Estotiland, 120, 160
Every, Henry, 69

Faeroe Islands, 22
Ferdinand, King, 48, 138–39, 140
Florence, Italy, 141–43
Florida, 58–59
Florin, Jean, 54, 55
Flynn, Errol, 123
France, 52, 54–57, 145–46
Francis I, King, 54, 55, 145–46,
    147–48, 148, *149*
Franklin, Benjamin, 105, 163, 168
Freemasonry, 92, 97–99, *98*, 168–69
  church and, 105–6
  new land for, 160–61
  retreat of, 173
  slavery and, 173–74
  South America and, 169–72
  thirteen colonies and, 161–65
French Revolution, 167, *168*

Gaulle, Charles de, 127
Gnostics, 153, 158–59
Gonçalvez Zarco, João, 131
Grand Lodge of London, 92
Great Britain, 7, 42, 52, 165–67
  informants for, 88–89
  Royal Society and, 89–90
  vilification of the corsairs, 84–86
  See also corsairs
Great Secret, 81–82, 99, 116, 176
Greenland, 109, 110
Guiscard, Roger de, 44
Gunn, James, 117, 119

Haggard, H. Rider, 113
Hancock, John, 161–62
Hanseatic League, 23
Hawkins, John, 61–62
Hawkins, William, 64
Henry II, 59
Henry IV of Bourbon, 52, 53
Henry the Navigator, 42, 129
Hiram, King, 113
Holy Grail, 176
Hornigold, Benjamin, 71

Hospitallers of St. John, 33, 39, 152–55

Huguenots, 57–60, 80, 158

Iceland, 110
imperialism, 84–85
India, 111–12
Indian Ocean, 67–68
Inquisition, *31*, 39
Invisible College, 104–5
Ireland, 42
Isabella, Queen, 48, 138–39, 140
Italy, 13, 13–14, 141–43

Jair al-Din, 48–49, 49
Jamaica, 66–67
Jefferson, Thomas, 168
Jerusalem, *27*, 28–29, 137
Jesuits, 155, 158
Jesus, 80–81, 175–76
Jews and Judaism, 136–38, 138–39
João II, King, 134–35, 136
John of Austria, 49
John the Baptist, 142
John XXII, Pope, 129
Jolly Roger, 44, 83
Joseph of Arimathea, 80–81

Kidd, William, 6, 67–70, *68*, 82, 123
Knights Hospitaller of Saint John, 24, *25*

Lafayette, Gilbert du Montier, 168–69
La Rochelle, 1–2, 41–44
Latin States, 26–27
Laudonnière, René de, 59
Levis, Henry de, 155–56
Lincoln, Abraham, 173–74
Livingston, Robert, 67
Llançá, Conrad de, 47
Llúria, Roger de, 47
Louis II of Hungary, 49
Louis VI, King, 33
Lovel, John, 61

Madariaga, Salvador de, 138–39
Madoc, 114
Magdalene, Mary, 80–81, 139–40, 149–50, 158–59
Mandeville, Geoffrey de, *26*
Marchena, Antonio de, 136
Martel, Charles, 81
Masonic Rite of York, 99, 101
Mediterranean, 8, 12, 13, 46–49
megalithic cultures, 109–11
Mehmet II, Sultan, 137
Menéndez de Avilés, Pedro, 57, 59
Merovingians, 81
Mings, Christopher, 65, 83
Miranda, Francisco de, 169, 170
Molay, Jacques de, 39, 41
Monroe, James, 174
Monte, Pietro del, 154
Moore, William, 68, 70
Moors, 47, 50–51, 128
Moreno, Mariano, 170
Morgan, Henry, 6, 65–67, 83
Muslims, 33, *34*

Narrazione Zeno, 119–20, 121–22
Natives, 118, 147, 148, 150
navigation, 1–2, 109–10, 165. *See also* voyages
Netherlands, 53
Newfoundland, 149–50
New Jerusalem. *See* Arcadia
Newport, Rhode Island, 141
Newton, Isaac, 104
New World, 51–54, 61, 108–9, 113–14, 161–65. *See also* Arcadia
Normandy, 22–23
Nova Scotia, 18, 117

Oak Island, 82, 118–19, 122–24
Ocracoke Island, 71–72
Olier, Jean-Jacques, 157–58
Order of Teutonic Knights, 23
Order of the Knights of Christ, 42

Order of the Knights of the Temple
   according to history, 27–33, *28–32*
   Columbus and, 134, 139–40
   conclusions about, 175–78
   founding of, 24–27
   Huguenots and, 57–60
   Judaism and, 136–38, 139
   lost fleet of La Rochelle and, 41–44
   New World and, 53–54, 160–61
   persecution and dispersion of, 37,
      39, 41
   pictured, *30, 32, 38, 40*
   piracy and, 58–60, 80–82
   Portugal and, 128–31
   rise to power, 33–37, *34, 36*
   sodomy charges against, 30
   stoneworkers and, 94–95, 97
   thwarted revenge of, 49–50
   transatlantic voyage of, 115–18
   treasure of, 118–19, 122–24
   vows of, 31

Paine, Thomas, 163
Palestine, 26–27
Paul, Vincent de, 157, 159
Pavillon, Nicolas, 157
Payns, Hugo de, 27, 30, 33
Perestrello e Moniz, Felipa, 131,
   132–33, 135
Pérez, Juan, 136
Pérez de Gusmán, Juan, 66
Perpinyá, Bartomeu, 47
Philip II, 49, 52–53, 62, *86*
Philip IV, 39
Phoenicians, 111–13
Pinello, Francesco, 136–37
pirates and piracy, 1–2
   America and, 51–54
   ancient roots of, 8–9
   buccaneers, 6, 54–57
   conclusions about, 175–78
   corsairs, 7, 60–80, 73–75, 84–86
   false images of, 7–8
   female, 89

   Huguenots and, *58–60*
   meaning of, 6–7
   in the Mediterranean, 46–49
   privateers, 7, 48, 165–67
   Templars and, 58–60, 80–82
   Vikings and, 17–22
   weaponry of, *56*
Pitt, William, 161
Plutarch, 112
Pompeius, 12–17, *14*
Portugal, 41–42, 74, 128–31
Poussin, Nicolas, *101*
Priory of Sion, 33, *35*
privateers, 7, 48, 165–67
Protestants. *See* Huguenots
Puerto Rico, 64

Quintanilla, Alonso de, 136

Rackham, Jack, 75–80
Raleigh, Walter, 86–88, *87*
Ramsay, Andrew, 103
Razilly, Isaac de, 154
Read, Mary, 76, 78–79, *79*, 89
Rhode Island, 147
Ribault, Jean, 59
Roberts, Bartholomew, 73–75, 89
Robert the Bruce, 42, 128
Roberval, Jean-François, 59
Roger II, 44, 128
Rogers, Woodes, 74–75, 83
Roosevelt, Franklin D., 123, 127
Roosevelt, Theodore, 174
Roque, Jean-François de la, *55*
Rosslyn Chapel, *43,* 103–4, *104*
Royal Navy, 88
Royal Society, 89–90
Russia, 22

Saint Lawrence River, 59
Sales, Francisco de, 157–58
San Martín, José, 169–72
Sannazaro, Jacopo, 146
Santángel, Luis de, 136, 138

Santiago de Cuba, 65
Santo Domingo, 63
Saracens, 46, 47
Sarah, 140
Schaw, William, 103–4
Scotland, 42–43, 103
Scottish Rite, 96, 102–3
Seneca, 133
silver, 57
Sinclair, Henry, 43, 115–16, 118–19, 121, 140
Sinclair, William, 103
slaves and slavery, 47, 61, 85, 88–89, 173–74
Solinus, Gaius Julius, 133
Solomon, 111–13
Sorel, Jacques, 57
South America, 169–72
Sovereign Order of Malta, 153–55
Spain, 7, 46–48, 50–51, 51–54, 85–86, 88–89, 128
Spanish Armada, 64
Sparta and Spartans, 10–11, 12
Stonehenge, 110
stoneworkers, 41, 92–93, 93–97
sugar, 131–32
Suleiman the Magnificent, 48, 49

Teach, Edward, 70–72, 72
Temple of Solomon, 29, 99, 117
Testu, Guillaume le, 59
Themistocles, 11
Tortuga, 54, 58
Toscanelli, Paolo dal Pozzo, 133–34
treasure, 118–19, 122–24. *See also* Great Secret
Trismegistus, Hermes, 142
Turks, 49–50
Tyrrhenian Sea, 13

United Provinces, 53
Urban II, Pope, 25

Vane, Charles, 75–76
Varangians, 22
Vatican, 1–2, 25, 39, 53–54, 58, 105, 178
Vaz Corte-Real, João, 114
Vaz Teixeira, Tristán, 131
Verrazano, Giovanni da, 141, 143, 146–48
Verrazano, Girolamo da, 148
Vikings, 17–22, *19–20, 21*
Vilarogut, Jaume, 47
Villahermosa, 65
Villegaignon, Nicolas de, 59
Vinland, 160
voyages
    of Cartier, 149–51
    megalithic navigators, 109–11
    to the New World, 108–9, 113–14, 115–24
    of the Phoenicians, 111–13
    See also Great Secret; navigation

Walpole, Robert, 105
War of Independence, 167
Washington, George, 105, 163–65, *164,* 168
Wayne, John, 123
women, 75–80, 89
Wren, Christopher, 104

Yánez Pinzón, Vicente, 47–48

Zeno, Antonio, 81–82, 116–17
Zeno, Carlo, 119–22
Zeno, Nicoló, 81–82, 115, 116–17, 119

Books of Related Interest

The Knights Templar in the New World
How Henry Sinclair Brought the Grail to Acadia
by William F. Mann

The Templar Meridians
The Secret Mapping of the New World
by William F. Mann

The Knights Templar in the Golden Age of Spain
Their Hidden History on the Iberian Peninsula
by Juan García Atienza

The Templars and the Assassins
The Militia of Heaven
by James Wasserman

An Illustrated History of the Knights Templar
by James Wasserman

The Mystery Traditions
Secret Symbols and Sacred Art
by James Wasserman

Founding Fathers, Secret Societies
Freemasons, Illuminati, Rosicrucians, and the Decoding of the Great Seal
by Robert Hieronimus, Ph.D., with Laura Cortner

Secret Societies of America's Elite
From the Knights Templar to Skull and Bones
by Steven Sora

Inner Traditions • Bear & Company
P.O. Box 388
Rochester, VT 05767
1-800-246-8648
www.InnerTraditions.com

Or contact your local bookseller